"There are lessons to learn here. We see that prayer is key to making things happen ... We see that perseverance in preaching the Word is essential ... We are reminded that there are corners of the world that we do not know about even though the world is shrinking. Missionaries are needed to preach the gospel in those places, and this book reveals just how much spiritual hunger there can be in those who have never heard."

Rico Tice, Senior Minister at All Souls Church, Langham Place, London

"John Butterworth's wonderful story about the life of the Albanian army officer Berti Dosti, shows us that God calls people from every possible background and changes their lives for ever. The story of what happened to Berti is as enthralling as a spy thriller. And it leaves the reader asking: If God can call people like this, might he be calling me too?"

Gordon Mursell, Former Bishop of Stafford

"This extraordinary story is a powerful testimony of the way that human beings need to worship. The God-implanted impulse to worship, found in every human heart, does not change whether it is confronted by militant atheism in Albania or, as in the case of much of the West, with materialism. John Butterworth's account of Berti Dosti's life will inspire Christians around the world to share their faith confidently in word and deed."

Alan Smith, Bishop of St Albans

GOD'S SECRET LISTENER

GOD'S SECRET LISTENER

JOHN BUTTERWORTH

10 Publishing
a division of 10 ofthose.com

First published in Great Britain in 2010 by Monarch Books

British Library Cataloguing in Publication Data
A record for this book is available from the British Library

ISBN: 978-1-914966-27-9

Designed and typeset by Pete Barnsley (CreativeHoot.com)

Image credits:
Albanian soldier, File ID 166166172 | © Cateyeperspective, Dreamstime.com
Albanian landscape; The approach to Thethi, Albania, by 45ossington – CC BY-SA 3.0

Printed in Denmark

10Publishing, a division of 10ofthose.com
Unit C, Tomlinson Road, Leyland, PR25 2DY, England

Email: info@10ofthose.com
Website: www.10ofthose.com

1 3 5 7 10 8 6 4 2

CONTENTS

FOREWORD

I can still remember the sense of excitement as my plane approached Tirana airport. The year is 1994 and the excitement is tinged with apprehension. Tirana was an airport without meaningful radar cover and the runway infamous for being cobbled! A very bumpy landing, a long wait to be let off the plane, and then down some rickety steps into a freezing winter night.

Once over the physical concerns, the political, cultural and spiritual questions filled my mind. What will life be like in this avowedly atheistic state? How will people be adapting to life now that the dictator, Enver Hoxha, is finally gone? Has the church survived and what does its future look like?

I discovered a land trapped in a 1940's time warp – economically impoverished, politically isolated and spiritually barren. And yet … God's people were still to be found! Small in number, lacking in leadership and bereft of resources ... but strangely peace-filled and certain of faith. It was thrilling to preach to a small group of believers on a Sunday in the Albanian capital – a wonderful demonstration of the resilience of the church under pressure, a living example of the fact that even the 'gates of hell' will not prevail against the Body of Christ!

It was with the backdrop of these experiences in Albania that I read this manuscript by John Butterworth. What a pleasure to read the inspiring story of Berti Dosti. A story of transformation, hope, conversion and mission. God is at work in individuals and nations, in Britain and in Albania ... no less in 2022 than in the first century.

May your faith be encouraged as you read this compelling salvation story.

Steve Gaukroger, Clarion Trust

PREFACE

For a long time, Albania lurked just within my radar. Initially I was no more than inquisitive about a nation that had banned religion and any semblance of Western influence and values.

Then Albania gradually moved more to the centre of my attention.

First because I found myself interviewing a young missionary who'd visited, as a tourist, to see how things were. She'd returned with details of an almost undocumented reign of terror that had set out to eradicate all places of worship and those who would wish to use them. She also told of her divine encounters with several maintaining their faith in secret and against all odds.

Then, for several years, I led Christian groups at a holiday centre in Corfu, directly opposite Albania. Here I'd led special prayer times looking across the sea between the two – thanking God for what we were sure he'd be doing by his Spirit there and asking for a day of freedom to come.

Our prayers were a mere fraction of those prayed both within Albania and round the world. And God did what God does. He answered and freedom came. Over the following months I heard first-hand accounts from those who were now sharing God's love in word and action – and seeing New Testament things happen as people came to faith and a fledgling church discovered how to fly.

All the while I was convinced, I knew only a fraction of what had gone on during the dark days of vicious persecution. God had been at work behind all our backs and one day it would be told. Now, this very important book draws back the curtain.

John Butterworth brings his considerable skill and experience as a journalist in order to both document and bring to life this remarkable account of how Captain Berti Dosti became Pastor Berti Dosti.

It is written with great attention to detail. And though this may focus on just one person and one story, through it you capture the even greater narrative of an amazing God who is on a mission.

The transformation that has come to Albania is nothing compared to the transformation God is bringing to lives there – as this valuable book reveals. Read, wonder, and enjoy.

Peter Meadows, Associate Director, Bible Society

INTRODUCTION

Most people have heard of evangelist Billy Graham, very few have heard of Billy Sunday.

Yet Billy Sunday has played probably just as important a part in Christianity as Billy Graham has.

In 1924, Billy Sunday ran a Christian campaign in Charlotte, USA, out of which came the Charlotte Businessmen's Club, who invited Dr Mordecai Ham to one of their meetings. He became a Christian at one of the rallies and ten years later, the club invited Dr Ham to lead another campaign, where a 16-year-old became a Christian in 1934. His name was Billy Graham.

It is interesting to trace back whom you have met on your life journey and what influences they have had on you, and I would encourage every reader of this book to do that.

For many people they are just meetings of coincidence, but Christians believe they are God-incidences and that

God brings people into contact for a purpose, such as to help someone discover Christianity.

Also, it is fascinating to trace back and see how many people over many years have been involved in bringing someone to faith.

One such person is Berti Dosti, who became a Christian even though he was a Communist captain in the Albanian Army. This closed country had a dictator, Enver Hoxha, who ruled with a rod of iron from 1941 until his death in 1985. He proudly declared in 1967 that his nation had 'abolished God' and it had become the world's 'first atheistic state'.

I first met Berti Dosti in May 2009 when I had been made redundant after 37 years in journalism and was wondering what to do next. I wrote to six charities I had supported all my life and offered to write for them for free. One of them invited me to go on a trip with them to Albania. I was delighted as I had always been intrigued by this country which had been cut off to the rest of the world for more than 40 years.

There I met the former Captain Dosti, and now Pastor Dosti. As I talked to him, I was staggered by how God spoke to Berti and the number of people He had used all over the world, and in the most unlikely places, to help bring him to faith, and this gave me the idea for this book.

Albania, or in Albanian Shqipëria, translated as the Land of the Eagle, had been a forgotten country, but when Hoxha died in 1985, it opened its borders again to the rest of the world. People began to take notice of it, especially when England drew Albania in the 1990 World Cup qualifying competition. But the English team was so suspicious about this secret country that they brought their own food, their own chef and flew home immediately after the away game in March 1989, which they won 2-0, Bryan Robson and John Barnes scoring the goals.

However, Albania, which is just north of Greece and across the Adriatic from Italy, is waking up after more than 40 years of living under probably Europe's cruellest and severest totalitarian regime.

The country, which has a surprising Christian heritage, has now gone from a dictatorship to a democracy, from a badly-resourced military force to a member of NATO, and from an isolated state without a friend in the world, to wanting to become a member of the European Union and from a closed country to an open one welcoming tourists.

This book is the journey of how Captain Berti Dosti became Pastor Berti Dosti against a backdrop of a radically changing country that is rejoining the world family.

I am indebted to many, many people on my own life journey and their help with this book.

I would like to thank Richard Tiplady, the former British director of the European Christian Mission, who sent me to Albania and started me on this fascinating project. Thanks to all at ECM (European Christian Mission) and all at Trans World Radio.

The book would not have happened without the help of Berti and Tatjana Dosti and translator Alma Syla who have all become close friends. It is amazing to think that if

I, as a journalist and Christian, had met Captain Berti some years ago in Albania he would probably have arrested me.

To be fluent in probably two of Europe's most difficult languages is no mean achievement, especially when Alma didn't learn English until her early-20s and mostly taught herself under candlelight at night.

I am also extremely grateful to my journalist colleague and sister-in-law Jackie Gregory, who cast a careful sub-editor's eye over the manuscript.

Finally, my eternal thanks to someone who inspired me to write the book, who gave me many constructive comments and ideas and who has been my best friend and closest companion on my own life's journey – my wife Jan.

1

IF YOU WANT TO FIND OUT MORE ABOUT GOD WE WILL MEET AGAIN TOMORROW

Berti Dosti faced a terrible but intriguing dilemma. He was an Albanian army captain and his job as a radio specialist was to listen in to the world's airwaves during the 1980s, as his country feared they were about to be invaded by the West, particularly by Russia, the USA and Britain. He was in the middle of a 24-hour shift and he was getting tired and bored, as he had had to do more than his fair share of duties recently. As he idly twiddled the radio dials, he heard a voice saying: "If you want to find out more about God we will meet again tomorrow."

Like all Albanians, 32-year-old Berti had been told God didn't exist and that anyone caught showing an interest in a Western radio programme and religion could expect a heavy punishment for not only them, but also on their family, their children and even their grandchildren. Still, something intrigued Berti. But how could he take up that invitation putting his whole family at risk and how could he listen in secretly when one in two Albanian army personnel was reckoned to be a government spy?

For five nights a week Trans World Radio, a Christian station in Monte Carlo, beamed a 15-minute programme in Albanian on 1467 kilohertz (kHz), 600 miles over Italy and across the Adriatic into this secretive country. Although these two places were only a few hundred miles apart and both were in Europe – in reality they were worlds apart.

Monte Carlo was a luxury resort, a tax exile and home of millionaires in the principality of Monaco in the south eastern Mediterranean corner of France, attracting the super rich, including film stars, gamblers or Formula 1 stars racing in the Monaco Grand Prix.

On the other hand, Albania, north west of Greece and opposite the heel of Italy, had a slightly different tourism policy – no visitors welcome under any circumstances. The nearest anyone had of reaching Albania in the 1970s and 1980s was if a sun worshipper on the nearby Greek island of Corfu on a boat happened to stray into Albanian waters. The watching Albanian military would quickly show them the error of their ways and force them back to their island beaches.

Since taking power in 1944, Enver Hoxha had turned Albania into the world's most isolated country, ruling it with Stalinist tyranny and fear. He was determined to wipe out religion, repeating a phrase taken from the 19th century Nationalist leader Pashko Vasa who said: "There is no religion in Albania, except being an Albanian."

This fanatical despot waged war on religion just as he had done with the Fascist Italian and German occupiers during the Second World War.

He destroyed churches or converted them into post offices, schools, weapon depots, cafes, barns, storehouses or museums. The cathedral at Shkodra was even turned into a volleyball court and in 1972, a museum of atheism was opened in the capital Tirana. For the last 23 years of his Communist rule there was not a single functioning church in the country. All 2,169 religious buildings, including mosques, Orthodox and Roman Catholic churches were closed. Of the country's 1,600 churches, monasteries and cultural centres in 1967, fewer than 80 were still standing 23 years later when communism ended in 1991.[1]

Many Orthodox priests and Christians were sent to prison, tortured and then executed by firing squad. During Hoxha's reign of terror, 335 Orthodox priests

---

1   *The Resurrection of the Church in Albania. Voices of Orthodox Christians.*
Jim Forest, WCC Publications.

died by execution, mistreatment, untreated illnesses or exhaustion. By the time it finished, only 22 Orthodox priests were still alive. All religious institutions were forbidden to have any connections or headquarters outside Albania, so the Roman Catholic Church had to cut its links with Rome and was designated instead as the Independent Catholic Church of Albania.

The constitution banned all "fascist, religious warmongerish, anti-socialist activity and propaganda". Prison sentences of between three and ten years were imposed for the possession of "religious propaganda and for the production, distribution or storage of religious literature."

Another decree targeted Christian names. Any citizen whose name did not conform to "the political, ideological or moral standards of the state" was required to change it. To help parents, the government published lists with pagan names to choose from, including newly-created names such as Marenglen (a combination of Marx, Engels and Lenin). A new girl's name, Enveriada, was invented in honour of Enver Hoxha, while his nicknames of Shpati and Tarasi also became accepted names for children.

Despite this, Albanians are proud of their history and believe they have a rich religious heritage.

In the Bible in Romans 15 verse 19, the Apostle Paul states: "So from Jerusalem all the way round to Illyricum, I have fully proclaimed the gospel of Christ."[2]

---

2   New International Version of the Bible.

Today the Roman Illyricum would be part of Albania, the Dalmatian coast, Kosovo, Bosnia and Herzegovina and Montenegro with the River Sava being the northern border.

The Catholic historian, Daniele Farlati, believes the Apostle Paul came to Albania.

He is supported by the theologian FF Bruce, who points out that in Acts 20 Paul travelled through Greece and there would have been time for him to call in to Albania. Because he travelled by ship round the Mediterranean it was likely that, to get to Thessalonica, he went along the Egnatian Way, which begins at Dyrrachium, the modern port of Durres in Albania, goes through Greece and ends in Constantinople (modern Istanbul).[3]

Some Albanian Christians believe Paul preached in the centre of Apollonia, a city 10 km from the eastern coast of the Adriatic Sea near Fier which flourished under Roman rule. Today many tourists visit these impressive ruins. Whether Paul stopped in Albania cannot be proved, but what is fact is that by AD 59, Dyrrachium had its first Christian bishop and up to 70 Christian families were living there.

Meanwhile, Berti had been taught Albanian history at school without the religious heritage. This made his

---

3   *The Message of Acts*, John R W Stott, *The Bible Speaks Today*, IVP, Page 316.

dilemma about a sudden interest in God much more difficult. He wanted to listen to the next night's Trans World Radio broadcast without anyone knowing. However, he knew if he was caught, he could be sent to jail, thrown out of the army and have his uniform taken off him. That would bring disgrace on his family. His father and his brother had both been soldiers; what would they think of his 'treason'? His party biography, or record of achievements, would mean nothing and he probably would never work again, or he would be sent away to a remote part of Albania. His wife and children would suffer, their party biography would be blemished, his children and grandchildren would not be allowed to go to university and they would all lose the privileges that being a good member of the party brought. Finally, it would bring an inglorious end to a brilliant military career for Captain Dosti, who was now in charge of his military base and who had already, at 29 years of age, been awarded the third highest military medal in Albania, one of the youngest ever winners of the Urdhri i Sherbimit Ushtarak te Klasit III.

As Berti pondered all this, he suddenly realised how he could listen in to that Trans World Radio programme and no one would know.

2

A PIONEERING SPIRIT

Being born into an army family was not easy for Berti who lived in six different homes all over Albania in the first ten years of his life. What made it more difficult for him was that his parents, Shefit and Antoneta, divorced when he was just three years old. He and his older brother, six-year-old Iliri, were split up and they never lived under the same roof again. Berti stayed with his father, an army officer, while Iliri went to live with an uncle, and neither of them saw their mother again for 30 years.

Berti was born on April 11, 1957, in Korçë, the regional capital of south east Albania and not far from the Greek border. However, he has few memories of his early years there, although he was to return to Korçë later in life on a very poignant mission.

Although out on a limb, the attractive town with interesting Ottoman buildings has played an important part in the country's rich religious and historical heritage.

One of its most famous residents was Gjerasim Qiriazi, a 19th century evangelical preacher and a pioneering educationalist who, with his sister, set up a school for girls in Korçë. In 1882, he started The Evangelical Brotherhood of Albania, to unite people to work for the good of the nation.

Another famous resident was the Albanian dictator Enver Hoxha. Although born in Gjirokastra on October 16, 1908, the son of a cloth merchant, he moved to the French Lycee in Korçë where he read French, history, literature, philosophy and the Communist manifesto.

Ironically, with a state scholarship given by the Albanian Queen Mother, he went to study biology at the University of Montpellier in France before moving to Paris where he joined the French Communist Party.

In 1936, he returned to Korçë to teach and helped found an underground Communist organisation. Following the 1939 Italian invasion, he was dismissed as a teacher for refusing to join the Albanian Fascist Party and then opened a tobacconist's shop, called Flora, in Tirana, where a small group of Communists began to gather, until the government closed it.[4]

4   *Blue Guide: Albania & Kosovo* by James Pettifer.

After the divorce, Berti and his father Shefit moved from Korçë to Kamez, near Tirana, for three years where Shefit's brother lived with his five children and who helped to look after Berti. However, when his father remarried, six-year-old Berti took a dim view of this, as did the military authorities. Within a few weeks, the family were sent to Sazan Island as a punishment because even in Stalinist Albania, divorce was frowned upon. Officers told recruits: "If you don't behave, you will be posted to Sazan Island."

This island is only four kilometres by five kilometres in the Bay of Vlorë off the south western corner of Albania. It has always been of strategic importance, occupied by the Italians before the First World War, an important Soviet base in the 1950s and housing United States military advisers to the Albanian Government in the 1990s.

Berti remembers the island, which is about a 45-minute boat ride from Vlorë, as a huge forest with a field in the middle where there was the military base and a small school for officers' children.

For a young boy growing up, there were plenty of places to explore. But as no one could leave this strategic island, which would probably bear the full force of any first assault if an enemy had ever attacked Albania, the novelty soon wore off.

Within two years, the grateful Dosti family were packing up again to drive to the north west of the country, near the Montenegro border, to Shengjin with its long sandy beach and a history of political intrigue.

Early in the 20th century, it had been the centre for international tension. Sir Harry Eyras, whose whitewashed house is still on the waterfront at Shengjin, was a former Lloyd's shipping agent who became a spy in the 1920s and was the first British diplomat to be resident in Albania.[5]

Berti lived there for less than a year in a condominium where he enjoyed beachcombing for seashells and collecting plastic bottles washed up on the beach. He kept his 'treasures' on a shelf by his bed – with the ultimate find being a Coca Cola bottle.

It wasn't long before Berti and family were off again in an army lorry and heading for nearby Lezha, a famous town housing the tomb of the Albanian hero Gjergjj Kastrioti Skenderbeu.

Skenderbeu, born in 1405, was the only one to survive when he and his three brothers were taken hostage by the Turks in 1423 and poisoned. Gjergjj joined the Turks' Ottoman army and did so well he was hailed 'Chief of the League of the Albanian People' and was given the name Skenderbeu, after Alexander the Great. He then re-converted to Christianity, changed sides and was named 'Champion of Christendom' by Pope Nicholas V for his battles with the Turkish invaders. He died in 1468 of fever and was buried in Lezha on January 17. However, when

---

5   *Blue Guide: Albania & Kosovo* by James Pettifer.

the Turks took the town they had their revenge, digging up his body in St Nicholas Church, dismembering it and making charms out of his bones. Today, a bronze bust of Skenderbeu stands on the nave floor of the church with replicas of a sword and of a helmet.[6]

By now, Berti was used to moving school and found it easy to make new friends.

He was very intelligent and he could soon adapt, as the syllabus was the same at all primary schools – writing, reading, a little Albanian history and geography, plus the most important subject, education which was studying what Enver Hoxha said and how Albanians should behave. Every day all pupils had to gather outside their school and a teacher would ask them: "Pupils and students at war, for the sake of the Party and the nation, are you ready?"

To which they would reply in unison: "Always ready."

Just 18 months later, Berti was again putting his possessions and treasures in an army van as the family headed a few miles south to the industrial town of Laç.

The most important occasion for Berti and all young Albanians was when they reached the age of nine and became Pioneers.

Berti remembers becoming a Pioneer, when the whole class was taken to the Place of the Heroes graveyard in

---

6   *Blue Guide: Albania & Kosovo* by James Pettifer.

Laç where they were lined up in front of the Albanian flag. This black double-headed eagle flag on a dark red background is one of the most ancient flags in Europe and very emotive to Albanians as it was Skenderbeu's flag when he fought for his country's independence.

When the National Assembly of Vlora proclaimed Albanian independence on November 28, 1912, they approved the flag as a symbol of their nation. The double-headed eagle shows their dual Christian heritage of the Western Catholic tradition and the Orthodox East. The horizontal open winged eagle also symbolises that Albanians will not submit to foreign conquest. When the Communists took control after the Second World War, they added a yellow, five-pointed star to the flag, but this was removed after independence in 1990.

The director of the school and the vice director asked the youngsters to swear allegiance before the flag. They would reply by promising "to give our lives, our last drop of blood for the Party".

Each pupil was presented with a special book, with their name, age and organisation number on it with a triangular red scarf symbolising the blood of the heroes who had given their lives fighting the enemy. It was considered a holy scarf, which they were expected to wear all the time. If they didn't, they were insulting the national heroes and their sacrifice. To ensure each student took their role seriously, each school had its own youth organisation and leader, usually one of the teachers.

Berti said you learnt at an early age to be careful what you thought and what you said. He said everyone, including children, were watched all the time and were observed on what they said. The state drew up a biography on all its citizens, and even comments by a relative or enemy could influence this.

If anyone ever misbehaved, they were asked: "Is this the behaviour our Party wants? Do you want to oppose the Party? Do you not want to honour the heroes?"

The ultimate discipline at every school was the threat to take away the scarf. If a young child went around without their scarf, it was obvious they had done wrong and so were ridiculed.

Other than the Pioneer ceremony, Berti remembers little of Laç, as every holiday he was sent all the way from north west Albania to the south east of the country to spend the summer with his stepmother's family at Melcan, a small farming community near Korçë. All young Albanian children had divided loyalties regarding their mothers. From an early age, they were taught: "I have two mothers. The first and the greatest one is the Mother Party and then my mother."

Although he went there for a number of holidays, he was never allowed to go back to the nearby town of his birth – his father did not want him to have any contact with his natural mother, Antoneta.

Ironically, the only time he did go to Korçë was when his stepmother's father took him for a treat on his horse to the town market. Suddenly, he went white and quickly turned the horse in the other direction and Berti saw a face in the crowd. To this day, he was convinced that was his real mother.

Berti thoroughly enjoyed his holidays there playing in the fields with his stepmother's four cousins and enjoyed looking after their cows and sheep. From the age of seven, all the village children went to the local primary school six days a week and then helped on the land on Sundays.

He didn't realise it then, but the second oldest of his stepmother's nieces, Tatjana, who lived in Melcan, was to play an important role in his life.

Also, when later in life he returned to Laç, it was in much more frightening circumstances.

3

WE'RE IN THE ARMY NOW

After ten years of moving around Berti at last had some stability to his life when at the end of December 1967, he, his father, stepmother and her daughter, were transferred to Lushnje, a medium sized industrial, lowland town. It would be a permanent move for Berti and also the start of a lifelong friendship with a neighbour's boy, Ladi.

Although the nine-year-old was a year younger than Berti they soon became close friends, especially as Ladi had a large house with a big garden, ideal for football, and hide and seek. He was at their house so often that he became almost part of Ladi's family.

They lived close to the town's most famous and historic house where the Congress of Lushnje was held in 1920 when an historic vote was taken by the Muslim, Catholic and Orthodox members for total national independence, the first town in Albania to do so.

In 1915 a secret treaty had been made by the European superpowers in London to split Albania between Greece and the then Yugoslavia. The Albanians sent representatives to the 1919 Paris Peace Conference to argue, understandably, against the move. The 1921 Conference of Ambassadors in Paris then recognised Albania as an independent sovereign state, apart from the area of Kosovo which then came under Yugoslav control. This caused a problem which would resurface more than 75 years later with the Kosovo War in 1998. It also led to a young tribal leader, Ahmet Zogu, returning from exile in Yugoslavia and being crowned King Zog on September 1, 1928.[7]

In Lushnje, Berti finished his primary school education and started his four years at secondary school, where he became interested in electronics and radios.

Being the son of an army officer, he had a privileged upbringing as the military had better salaries and houses than ordinary Albanians, plus some free groceries. Berti lived in a two-bedroomed house with a kitchen, good furniture, TV but with Albanian programmes only, and a fridge. Berti was fortunate; many thousands of Albanians had a much tougher time.

---

7   *Blue Guide: Albania & Kosovo* by James Pettifer.

Typical of those was Alma Syla, who was born in Lushnje in 1972, and who Berti was later to employ as an English teacher at his school.

Alma and her two brothers were born to Mustafa and Ervehe, who worked for the Government in the collective farming fields, earning very little money. They lived in a three-roomed house, consisting of a bedroom, a kitchen and a tiny bathroom. One of Alma's brothers slept in the bedroom with his parents, while she and her other brother slept in the kitchen. The family couldn't afford to buy beds, so their father made them out of spare wood and plastic strips. The only other furniture was a table, a bench and a couple of chairs, and one cupboard. There was no tap in the kitchen; the only one was in the bathroom along with a sink and a toilet. It was not until 1987, when Alma was 15, that the family could afford to buy their first TV.

Alma's parents left the family home six days a week at 6am to walk for around 30 minutes to arrive at the fields and start work at 6.45am. They had just an hour for lunch and didn't return home until 6pm.

The workers were allowed to eat vegetables from the fields for their lunch and many put extra veg in their bags to take home for their families.

"The authorities realised what was going on, but they turned a blind eye," said Alma. "They knew that the workers were so poor that if they didn't allow it some of them would starve to death."

When their mother returned home, she made the family their only hot meal of the day, a vegetable dish. Meat was scarce and a luxury. Alma remembers being asked one year, what she would like for her birthday and she replied "some meat".

She said there was often so little food in the house that for breakfast she had just bread with water to soften it and some sugar on top. Some days she went to school, from 7.30am until 1.30pm, without any breakfast. When Alma returned home, she would play games in the road with her friends until her mother came back from the fields.

Although school and medical treatment was free, parents had to pay to send their children to university and for medicines. Many families had to spend all their money on providing food and Alma knew of adults who would regularly sell their own blood so they could pay the extra bills.

However, there were some disadvantages for army families with Berti's father having to work away for days and weeks on end. With transport difficult and many of the bases isolated it was difficult to go anywhere, that is once you had permission to leave camp.

"We did not know what life was like in the outside world. We thought our life was normal," said Berti.

After becoming a Pioneer at nine, Berti then joined the Youth Organisation from 14 until 18 when every Albanian student had to spend a month every summer, including Sundays, working in the fields.

One summer Berti and the rest of his school were taken to the village of Plug, a 10-minute bus ride away from Lushnje. When they arrived, there were about 800 students, and the 80 teachers divided the fields up so each pupil had three lines of corn to harvest. Berti and the other teenagers were left to cut the tall corn with their own hands and peel away the dried leaves.

It was hard work; the weather was warm and Berti soon got bored. With the corn taller than the students it was easy to hide, so Berti and two friends spent a pleasant morning chatting – until a male teacher discovered them. He lashed out at them, hitting and kicking them so much 14-year-old Berti decided to leave the secondary school for good.

Fortunately, his father was away with the military for a month and his stepmother didn't know what Berti was doing. When his father returned home, it was too late for Berti to enrol for that year. There was a huge row as he accused his son of being a 'bad boy', the ultimate disgrace for Albanian families. His father then went to see the school, and the teacher and parent agreed that Berti should return to school the following year.

In the meantime, he joined the building trade for six months, a job he said was hard work, but it gave him some independence and taught him much about electrics, which was to prove very useful.

The following April his father persuaded Berti to go instead in the following September to Durres High School, a technical academy. It meant Berti leaving Lushnje to go to the port of Durres, an hour and a half's journey away. Although his father had to pay, it gave Berti the chance to complete a diploma as an electric technician, which would eventually lead to a career.

When he left the technical college four years later, he returned to Lushnje full time to work for an electrical company for a month before being tempted by the big industrial complex of Elbasan – and the prospect of better pay.

Enver Hoxha had left a lasting legacy on the whole of Albania, but the town that probably changed the most under him was Elbasan.

This former Roman fortress town was one of the most pleasant and unspoilt Ottoman cities in Albania with its narrow, cobbled streets, historic buildings and public gardens.

It was then developed as an industrial centre by the Communists with Chinese assistance in the 1960s and 1970s, leaving Hoxha to call it 'the second national liberation of Albania'.

The huge 'Steel of the Party' metallurgical complex outside the city complex was turned into a pollution nightmare. With its chimneys, the tallest in the Balkans, belching out smoke and dangerous pollutants into the atmosphere, it soon destroyed the prosperous agricultural area.

However, one of the most infamous buildings to survive is a yellow bungalow, 6 Rr Universitetit, the home of a widow, Peggy Hasluck, who during the Second World War was a Special Operations Expert. She briefed British officers parachuted in to help the Albanian resistance movement while having a love affair with an Albanian clan leader, Lef Nosi.[8]

Berti didn't see much of the town; he worked officially eight hours a day with Sundays off. But, like all the other workers there, he did as much overtime as possible and always worked his day off, helping put electric lines into the new steel factory ovens.

All the equipment came from China and there were many Chinese specialists overseeing the project. Berti was there when Enver Hoxha fell out with Chairman Mao and the Chinese experts were forced to leave the country. To China's surprise, the Albanians took over the work, quickly adapted the equipment and ensured the plant continued without their help.

When his year's contract in Elbasan ended in June 1978, Berti returned to Lushnje and his old electrical company

8   *Blue Guide: Albania & Kosovo* by James Pettifer.

and where he made two important decisions. Firstly, his father persuaded him to join the army and secondly, he became engaged.

As Berti's brother Iliri had enlisted in the army, it was expected that Berti would follow in the family tradition. Only one person per family was allowed to go to university for free, so while Iliri had studied as an officer, Berti had to work his way up the ranks.

Despite his laziness in the cornfield, Berti still had a good party biography.

Therefore, it was no surprise that, with his family record, his industrial experience and being a youngster who enjoyed gymnastics, he was given an interview to join the army, which was a great success. On September 1, 1978, he reported to Tirana Military School for two years' intensive training – with no holidays.

Because of his interest in radios, he was put in the communications group, with about 30 other military trainees. "Although I wasn't one of the strongest physically in the group, I made up for it because I had worked in industry and was a little older," said Berti.

His father also had a bearing on the second important decision that year for Berti. Even in the 1970s and 1980s, arranged marriages were the norm in Albania, although it is much less common now.

His father said he had had discussions with the family and he would like Berti to consider marrying Tatjana Dervishi, his stepmother's niece from the village of Melcan where Berti had spent many of his summer holidays as a youngster.

Tatjana's father, a chief accountant, was a Communist although, like his wife, he had been brought up to follow Bektashi, a little-known strain of Islam, founded by a Persian, Haji Betas Veil, in the 13th century.

In Albanian tradition, a younger brother had to discuss the marriage arrangements with his older brother to get his agreement before talking to his bride-to-be. Having got his brother's consent, both families gathered to celebrate the engagement on September 2, 1980. In the following autumn Berti and Tatjana were married in Melcan on Saturday, October 24, 1981.

His childhood friend, Ladi, played a vital part in getting Berti to the ceremony on time. Ladi's father was a tailor who made the bridegroom's wedding suit, but he was so busy that, after making the final adjustments, there wasn't much time for Berti to catch the train from Lushnje to Korçë.

With all the heavy rain that Saturday and puddles everywhere, Berti didn't want to get his new suit muddy. So Ladi carried him the 700 metres from his home to the railway station – on piggyback.

Tatjana, who married in a white wedding dress, said it was a memorable day. There were more than 100 guests in the village hall for the Saturday night event, which lasted six hours and included food, drink and dancing. There were no bridesmaids and no wedding photographs. The only wedding photograph Tatjana has of her and her new husband was taken in a studio three weeks later – in black and white.

This contrasted greatly with the wedding of Berti and Tatjana's daughter, Alta, on September 11, 2005. Alta, who was then 22, chose her own husband, 27-year-old Lenci Mene, who was born in Gjirokaster, the son of an army officer and an accountant. They met at a student camp in Sarande, and as they were both Christians, they were married in a church on a Sunday at 9am.

Alta wore a white dress and had three bridesmaids and more than 100 friends and family attended the service. This was followed by a reception at 11am in a Lushnje restaurant to which the couple were taken in a luxury car. During the reception, messages from friends all over the world were relayed on to a large screen and enough colour wedding photographs were taken to fill a large album. Afterwards, the couple flew off for a honeymoon in Turkey.

But what did Tatjana think of the two contrasting marriages? "At my own wedding," said Tatjana, "I was more worried about how the reception would go. But at Alta's wedding, I was more worried how the ceremony would go, as we were now a Christian family."

As for her own wedding, she said everyone respected their parents' authority.

What did she think of the two families' choice of her bridegroom?

"I was very, very happy with that," she said blushing slightly.

To which Berti chipped in: "All Albanian girls say that, particularly in front of their husband."

4

OFFICER MATERIAL

Berti didn't really want to be promoted to an officer in the Albanian Army. However, he and Tatjana had been married for two years and they now had a daughter, Alta, born on February 28, 1983, so money was tight. For the last two years, since leaving military school, he had been working back in Lushnje repairing radios, mainly for the army, and he was enjoying himself.

However, the salary for an army radio technician was quite low and there were no promotion prospects. In addition, his father and brother expected him to become an officer, so he agreed to apply.

Even in Communist Albania, it was not what you knew, but who you knew. His father, Shefit, who had a fine military record, sent a request to the high command for Berti to become an officer.

Shefit had started his military career by volunteering as a 14-year-old to help the Partisans during the Second World War. Although too young to fight the Italian and German invaders, he became a messenger boy for the Partisans.

When in 1941 Germany invaded Russia, and at the same time turned Albania into a puppet state, the Communist Party in Albania decided it was now a just war because it was anti-fascist. The party's main figure was Enver Hoxha who helped set up a countrywide National Liberation Movement, which in 1943 was expanded into a National Resistance Army (nicknamed the Partisans).

The Germans drove the Partisans into the mountains where they fought a guerrilla war. The only country to help them was Britain, who provided weapons, ammunition and clothing, which were delivered by parachute at night. Then the messengers, including Berti's father, delivered them to the Partisans.

When the war ended for Albania in late 1944 young people, including Berti's father, flocked to join the army full time. Hoxha turned the national liberation movement into a Communist revolution, much to Britain's horror who were hoping for a democratic government.

Ironically, it was British aid and arms, not Russian nor Chinese support, which helped Hoxha to power.

David Smiley, who worked for British Intelligence and who had liaised with Albanian resistance groups, had been puzzled that his reports and requests failed to get through to the Special Operations Executive. After the war, he was again shocked when details of a secret operation to train non-Communist Albanian troops outside Albania to resist Hoxha appeared to be known to the dictator. It was some time later before Britain realised that it was the infamous spy turned traitor, Kim Philby, who had later defected to Russia in 1963 who had been betraying British secrets over Albania.[9]

Because Berti was highly qualified with three diplomas and because of his family's record, he didn't have an interview to be an officer. The next day, August 6, 1983, Berti was told to report to the Sulzotaj garrison, which was west of Lushnje on the Adriatic coast.

At that time, Albania was continually on high military alert. It was so isolated having fallen out in turn with its three allies, Yugoslavia, Russia and China. Berti said the military were particularly worried about an invasion by the West.

The leaders were so paranoid that if an American warship passed near the Albanian coast on its way through the Adriatic the whole country was put on full military alert.

Hoxha also fell out with Britain, soon forgetting the help it had received from them during the war.

---

9   *Blue Guide: Albania & Kosovo* by James Pettifer.

In an episode known as the Corfu Channel Incident, which were really three early Cold War clashes, floating mines struck two British destroyers, the HMS Saumarez and the HMS Volage, on October 22, 1946, causing 44 deaths and 52 injuries. The Albanians claimed the British ships had strayed into their territorial waters, but the International Court of Justice at The Hague ruled the British case was legitimate. Albania refused to pay any compensation, so Britain impounded Albanian gold reserves in the Bank of England in London, and it took 46 years to resolve the dispute when the British authorities lifted the ban in 1992.[10]

Berti's job, as an expert in radios and communications, was to scan the airwaves for any hint that an enemy was approaching. He also was in charge of communications between the guns and gunners so that they could be moved to the correct position when an enemy was detected, and he was the link with the command centre in case of an attack. Finally, he oversaw all radio, telephone and signals communications within the base, including using couriers if necessary.

On top of that, every year for three months he had to teach the new conscripted soldiers how to use radios. The

---

10 *Blue Guide: Albania & Kosovo* by James Pettifer.

rest of the time was spent planning for an invasion and how the Albanians would respond.

Berti said they had hours of studying maps, planning war games on a table and thinking through every scenario.

He had to help answer questions from superiors, such as: What about food? What about transportation? If the enemy attacked point X, how would we respond? What if they attacked point Y, or even point Z?

"We got bored. It was always the same thing, meetings about war game meetings, it was so unreal," recalled Berti.

However, five days a month it did become more real as they carried out war scenarios moving equipment around, going through the procedures with different military passwords each time.

"After that," said Berti, "it was practising for the next practice."

Nevertheless, what it did show was that their Chinese and Russian radios were not that reliable. They had to keep changing frequencies so they could get a signal, and he knew that countries like Italy had far more sophisticated radios and that the Albanian military wouldn't be able to hold off an enemy for long. So, Berti ensured that when all their communications were knocked out, he still had human couriers to continue any war effort.

With all these long hours of boredom, did he ever wonder if an enemy existed?

"Yes, I did," said Berti, "especially as I never ever came across a foreign and dangerous signal.

"However, I only thought it. To doubt out loud the existence of an enemy and to worry that we might lose a war was unpatriotic and totally unthinkable."

He kept these thoughts to himself during the next three years as he moved up the command structure to be head of the base.

With Enver Hoxha in charge, everyone in communist Albania was supposedly equal and no soldiers officially had any ranks – that is apart from Enver Hoxha who was General Colonel of the Albanian Army and General Commandant of the Albanian Army.

Army ranks were abolished officially until 1990, but even before then everyone knew what rank soldiers were, particularly when they lined up for an official photograph and the leaders were on the front row.

Berti added: "We thought we were all equal, and we believed it. But what was said in Albania was different to what happened."

5

TEARS AS ENVER HOXHA DIES

Thursday, April 11, 1985, was the day Albanians and many Albanian watchers abroad will never forget. The people were shocked to be told that their leader, Enver Hoxha, had died aged 76, especially as they had no idea that he had been ill for the last couple of years with diabetes. His illness was a state secret; the few people who knew about it could have been sent to jail, or even put to death, had they divulged the information to anyone.

At the time, Berti was working at the Sulzotaj base near Fier and because he was an officer, he was able to live at home most of the time with his family in Lushnje.

That Thursday began as a normal day when he left at 5am to catch the military bus. As an officer, he worked

8am to 4pm six days a week and alternate Sundays, plus sleeping over at the base two or three times a week.

When Berti arrived at 7.30am, he noticed immediately a different atmosphere. No one spoke, there was silence everywhere and everyone kept their heads bowed, as though they didn't want to catch anyone's eyes and have to talk.

All the officers were called immediately to the Commandant's office for a meeting. "He was very solemn, very emotional and trying to fight back the tears," recalled Berti.

The Commandant said he had received a secret coded message from the Albanian Government adding: "I have some bad news to report, but you have to keep it secret." He then told them that Enver Hoxha had died.

"Everyone at the base cried, even I did," admitted Berti. "It was a case of the more a person cried the more it honoured our leader. Looking back now, I laugh at how much I cried."

Half an hour later at every factory, school, office and collective farm throughout the country, the local party secretary called the people together. By now, everyone knew something had happened because there was sombre music on the radio, but few guessed what it was.

Alma Syla, then a 13-year-old pupil, was with the other students in her class, working in the fields.

They had to have four lessons a week learning how to grow crops.

The youngsters knew something was up that Thursday morning because their teacher had stayed in the corner of the field crying and talking to one of the supervisory teachers. However, it wasn't until 9.30am that she called the students across.

In between tears, she sobbed: "Our beloved leader, our greatest person, is no more."

After announcing the news, she told the students to stop working, go home and report to school the next day. They were encouraged to watch TV where films of Hoxha's life were shown, and many tributes were paid to the leader against a backdrop of funereal music.

"Almost every one of us cried," recalled Alma, "including myself. We were frightened; we didn't know what was going to happen next. We believed Enver Hoxha had made our country secure, a strong castle, that no one would attack. But what would we as a country be like now without a leader?"

Back at the military base, the country was put on the highest military alert and the volunteer force was told to be ready for immediate call-up. The national leaders were worried that the army might lose its discipline, that external enemies might seize the opportunity to attack

Albania, or that internal enemies might lead an uprising and overthrow the government.

Berti said there were special organisations within the army and government to ensure there was no internal revolt, as many intellectuals would be glad to see the end of Hoxha's regime. "But they celebrated in silence," said Berti, "and they cried in public, as there were so many spies watching them to see their reaction."

Berti said his job, like all the military, was to prepare for an external attack, now that Hoxha had gone.

"We were told the enemy had not attacked us before because they realised our strength," he added, "and we believed the Party's word because we thought that they would never lie to us."

Albania was certainly prepared to defend itself. They had built nearly a million pillboxes or bunkers, which scarred the face of the country like concrete acne, from where they would try to repel the invaders with their machine guns. Also under every home, school, office and collective farm were tunnels where people could go.

"There was a national saying," recalled Berti, "which said, 'we are three million Albanians; we are three million soldiers ready to die to protect our achievements'."

From the age of 15 every student, boy and girl, had to spend four weeks every year, for four years, going to the hills for military training.

After leaving high school, all boys had to do two years' military service, or three years if they were sent to join the Marines on Sazan Island. All citizens also had to have four weeks' military training every year until they were 55 years old. Even then, they were expected to help with civil defence. Only children under 14, mothers with babies and retired people could go into the tunnels in the event of an attack, and they all had a specific place and plan. Those over 55 years old were expected to be first aiders, nurses, or food providers to those in the tunnels.

Many tunnels were small and self-contained like Second World War air raid shelters in England, while some were inter-connected, and others were like small underground towns with communication centres and hospitals for the country's government and military leaders.

Every so often bugles were sounded all over the country to test the people's readiness, and they would have to drop everything and take up their military positions. The Government would also report to the nation any border incidents, which happened sometimes in the south with Greece, as a warning of the military dangers.

With the country on the highest alert, Berti's first job was to check all his radios were working, particularly those connected to the four commanders who were looking after the Lushnje zone. He was very satisfied to find every radio and link was working perfectly. Next, he opened up all the communications on all the radios, which for most of the time were closed down, and checked all the orders and communication codes were ready. Finally, he ensured all the weapons at the base were in working order.

Next day, Friday, April 12, Alma and all the students throughout the country reported back to school. She said the normal uniform was a black dress and a white tie, but they had all taken off their ties as a mark of respect.

"First, our teacher tried to read the newspapers to us," said Alma, "but she cried so much she asked one of my friends to finish reading the articles. I couldn't believe she made my friend read those words."

A week of national mourning was declared and every school opened a book for pupils to submit their poems and songs about Enver Hoxha with the teachers deciding which were the best ones.

"Thousands and thousands of people wrote poems," said Alma, who had one of hers selected for her school's book.

"We all promised that we would continue to walk in Enver Hoxha's steps and we would never betray his ideal."

"Others wrote 'why did he die, Albania so needed him. I wish I could have died instead of him'."

That same day Hoxha's body was laid in state in Tirana and thousands of people travelled by buses and trains from all over Albania, despite the few forms of transport, to form an orderly queue and walk through the military guard of honour to pay their respects.

Although Berti wasn't called upon for military duty in Tirana, he stayed at his base as the country remained on high alert for the next five days.

However, the country continued to honour their leader with his birthday, October 16, being renamed Enver Hoxha Day, which then became an Enver Hoxha week.

The leader's daughter, Primavera, designed the Enver Hoxha memorial which opened in 1988 in the centre of Tirana on the 80th anniversary of his birthday. The dramatic structure, which was nicknamed the Pyramid because of its similarity to the Egyptian buildings, contained everything connected with the leader's life. In the centre was a huge marble statue of the leader himself.

Berti will never forget Thursday, April 11, 1985, and not just because of Hoxha's death – it was his 28th birthday.

"It was the strangest birthday of my life," recalled Berti. "Outside of my family no one knew it was my birthday and no one, including myself, dared celebrate it."

However, the Albania story was also unfolding 2,000 miles away. Stephen Bell, a grammar school educated Lancashire lad, an avid Manchester City fan and a vicar's son, who felt called to go to Albania, was spending Easter on a house party with a missionary group, the European Christian Mission, at their headquarters, Heightside in Rawtenstall, Lancashire. He was home on holiday from Prishtina University in Kosovo, where he was studying Albanian and waiting for the borders to open. Next morning on Thursday, April 11, at 7.30am, he again prayed and asked for a clear sign from God that he was meant to go to Albania.

Then, as he normally did every day, he switched on for the 8am news on Radio 4 and the first item was the announcement of the death of Enver Hoxha. "I knew then I was going to Albania," said Stephen.

But what was the European Christian Mission and how did they become interested in Albania?

That story began more than 100 years ago in a remote part of the Russian empire with the Raud family from Estonia.

6

FROM RUSSIA WITH LOVE

Christmas 1903 was a severe winter in Estonia, which was then a backwater of the Russian Empire ruled over by Tsar Nicholas II. However, that didn't stop Pertel Raud, a landowner who had been converted to Christianity when he was 26 by reading the Bible, from taking two of his sons on a 10-day preaching tour in his country.

A huge economic gap existed between the lifestyle of the rich aristocracy and the crushing poverty experienced by the common people. The powerful Orthodox Church persecuted "dissenters". At the end of the 19th century, a revival within the Lutheran Church in Scandinavia had touched the Baltic States. Even so, for Protestants to preach the gospel in places such as Estonia was to invite trouble, with meetings broken up and preachers arrested, while believers faced intimidation and discrimination.

However, that didn't put the Raud family off and on New Year's Eve, 1903, they came to a town where a meeting had been arranged in a large private house. The plan was for Pertel to speak first, followed by son Wil and then 25-year-old Ganz, the youngest of the five sons, would be last.

The meeting, which had started at 8pm, had gone well and it was quite late when Ganz got up to preach on The Judgment of the Great White Throne.

Just as he started the house was raided by the secret police come to arrest the preachers.

Before they took the trio away, amazingly, the police allowed Ganz to finish his sermon.

The police captain was so challenged by Ganz's preaching that he was converted and the other officers left without making any arrests.

The police captain wasn't the only one converted that night, 39 others were and a number of the believers there were so thankful that they agreed to spend the rest of the night in prayer.

It was in the early hours of 1904 that Ganz felt called to serve God in Europe and he looked back on that evening and morning as the beginning of the work he was later to start, the European Christian Mission.

Born in 1878 he became a Christian when he was 10 years old and he soon learnt to stand up for his faith despite the jeers and taunts of other boys at boarding school. His mother used to give him a new Bible every year and he had always read it from cover to cover by the time the next new one arrived.

"When I was 18," he recalled in *Sharing Christ's Love in Europe*[11], "I stood at a crossroads. Some friends urged me to pursue academic training, but my father and others were praying that my life might be given to the Lord's work, not the things of this world."

Over the next four years, he spent more time preaching, giving out tracts and visiting hospitals. He felt a burden for Europe, and in particular Great Britain, and North America. One day Ganz received an unexpected invitation to hear a German Bible teacher speak in a baron's castle in Tallinn, the capital of Estonia. The teacher encouraged Ganz to leave Estonia and offered him financial support to get more Bible training. Just as Ganz was planning to leave Estonia, he became so ill that he heard the doctors and his family discussing his funeral.

He recovered, but that wasn't the end of the problems. Some older Christians thought he was too young to go abroad and gave him money for his return fare home.

However, he was determined to go and left early in 1904, an opportune time as a General Strike was soon to sweep throughout Russia and revolution was in the air.

---

11 *Sharing Christ's Love in Europe*, published by ECM International 2004, Editor David Clark

To ensure he wasn't tempted to come back home, he quickly spent the money given for his return ticket.

For the next ten years, he travelled extensively in Europe setting up interdenominational prayer groups wherever he went.

In June 1904, he arrived in England to see first hand the effects of the Welsh Revival.

In the summer of 1914, three weeks before the outbreak of war, Ganz went to the Russian Consul in Berlin to renew his visa. Aware that war was imminent, the consul advised him to return to Estonia at once. There his brother Wil and his father continued to encourage their Estonian congregations to build mission halls, known as "Prayer Houses", and even the Sunday school children were involved in making bricks. Despite this, the family felt that Ganz should go to America to tell the needs of Europe to Christians there. After he was granted a passport, he set out on the hazardous wartime journey to America, via Sweden, Norway and England.

Both father and son knew they would probably never see each other again on earth so it was a poignant farewell at the railway station.

Ganz recalled: "On the train my father lifted up his hands and like a patriarch gave me his blessing. His last words were: 'God will lead you and keep you, my son, wherever He sends you. Be of good cheer. Let your life be always well pleasing to Him. Let Jesus be the first and last in everything; do not seek riches, or honour, or glory from men; seek only God's glory and the salvation of souls'"

With that, Ganz left Estonia in February 1915, and never saw his father again.

Pertel Raud died in 1918.

Ganz sailed for America on one of the last journeys of the Lusitania, reaching New York where he knew nobody. However, at a Bible study in the city, he met a young couple, Mr and Mrs Thomas McDonald, and it led to a lifetime of service together. Together they founded a mission, which they registered as the Russian and Slavonic Bible Union as Ganz's work then was mainly among Slavic people. It had three aims: Ministry in Europe, training courses to prepare candidates for working in Europe and a printing press to produce literature. In 1921, the name of the Bible Union was changed to the European Christian Mission and in 1922, the mission headquarters moved to Brooklyn, New York, where in 1924, Ganz married one of the mission staff, Miss Elsa Overton, a gifted writer and Bible teacher.

In 1927 Ganz visited England to register the mission rented offices, firstly in London and later at a house in Beulah Hill.

The post-First World War map of Europe had changed dramatically with old dynasties swept away and nine new countries appearing almost overnight. There were new opportunities in Central Europe, and the work of ECM began to expand.

At first ECM concentrated on providing food and clothing and then Bibles to countries such as Russia. By 1923 there were 55 ECM missionaries working in ten European countries. Within four years this had grown to 81 missionaries, 243 national helpers working in 132 meeting halls and thousands being converted. Today in 2022 ECM International has 216 missionaries working in 25 countries.

In Ganz's annual mission report in 1937 he said work was growing in Spain, France, Austria, Czechoslovakia, Poland, Estonia – where his brother Wil had been the mission director until he died in 1935 – Germany and the Soviet Union.

Like his father, Ganz had a special burden for the Jews and in the years leading up to the Second World War new workers were appointed to work among Jews in Austria, Hungary and Lithuania. Ganz was asked to speak at a Jewish synagogue in Eastern Europe as long as he didn't mention the name of Jesus. So, he preached on the Lamb of God.

When their London HQ was bombed during the war and the training centre in Penarth, South Wales, was too small to accommodate the growing number of students preparing to go to Europe, the mission contacted all their supporters saying they were looking for new premises.

One of them mentioned Heightside, near Rawtenstall, Lancashire, formerly the home of a Lancashire businessman and now a Christian conference centre and guesthouse.

Six years later in 1953 saw the close of one chapter and the opening of another.

Despite recent ill health Ganz Raud felt strong enough to begin a trip to Europe in the late summer. After visiting five countries, he arrived exhausted in Paris. On Saturday, October 3, having suffered a heart attack, he was found unconscious with his head resting on his own Bible open at Psalm 143. He later died in hospital.

The same year Heightside became the rented headquarters of ECM in Britain and eight years later, they took it over when Colonel Bolton, the original owner, gave it to the mission.

With its move to Rawtenstall ECM expanded its work, introducing an annual Easter conference at Heightside.

In 1961, ECM decided the best way to preach the gospel to those countries behind the Iron Curtain was by radio. When Hoxha declared Albania was the world's first atheistic state in 1967, it galvanised some Christians into sending Christian programmes from the Rawtenstall studio to Trans World Radio in Monte Carlo, where they were beamed into 'godless' Albania, with the first one transmitted on July 5, 1968. One of their many secret listeners would be Captain Berti Dosti, and two of the people who would play a major part in his spiritual journey were Stephen Bell and his friend Gani Smolica. But how did Stephen and Gani become involved in Albania?

7

WE BOTH CHANGED
EACH OTHER'S LIVES

Few students would put Prishtina University in Kosovo, Yugoslavia, in their list of top ten places in the world where they would like to study.

Surrounded by 300-metre hills Prishtina, the state capital, is in a valley with towering ugly 1960s concrete buildings, boring blocks of flats and chaotic traffic problems. Amazingly, the university has 60,000 students out of a population of 200,000.

But Prishtina can be a forbidding place with tensions between the Serbs and the majority Albanians just below the surface. When Albania had been declared an independent but smaller sovereign state under international guarantee in 1912, more than half the Albanians were left outside the new borders in places such as Kosovo, which had now become part of Yugoslavia.

Sometimes the tension came out into the open with the most serious leading to the Kosovo War in 1991.

An unusual student who arrived there on August 14, 1986, was Stephen Bell, who hardly spoke a word of Albanian and so couldn't understand much of the lectures. It didn't help that sometimes the lecturers moved rooms at the last minute and he couldn't translate the scruffy notes put on the doors telling students of the new location.

Dates and times of exams were another problem. University authorities didn't like to reveal them until the last possible minute which didn't help Stephen in his revision nor his holiday plans to go home to England.

In addition, 27-year-old Stephen, who had enrolled in the linguistics and philosophy faculty for five years, was also different to the other students – many of whom were Greek students dodging military call-up. Not only was he older than most of them, he did his best to fail the exams. This was so his visa could be renewed as a student and he could stay in Prishtina as long as possible to improve his language skills.

When Stephen told the other students he was hoping to go and work in Albania they all laughed and said: "There is no hope of Albania opening up to foreigners."

The real reason he was there was that he was a missionary working with ECM following up listeners to

Albanian radio broadcasts, as well as learning Albanian. As he wouldn't be allowed into the country if he put missionary on his visa application, he put student. But to do that he needed to stay at the university.

However, no matter how hard he tried to fail the exams, the authorities, who were mystified by Stephen whom they thought must be a spy, still gave him exam passes.

The police interrogated his friends asking them: "Who is Stephen? What is he doing here?"

Between July and August 1990, Stephen was aware of 11 of his friends who had been called in for questioning, though he wonders how many more were quizzed and didn't tell him. Stephen also knew his phone was bugged and his mail was opened.

Bizarrely, on his course Stephen had to take a second language – they tried to make him learn German – and when he plumped for Serbo-Croatian as it was at least of some practical use he was told he couldn't do that because it wasn't a foreign language. So, he had to study English and he even had to take an exam in it in his second year. Not surprisingly, Stephen did so well he ended up giving the lectures.

Finally, Stephen, who is still proud of his pass in Marxism, decided the only way to ensure he failed was not to turn up for some of the exams. By doing this he managed to stay there for five years before completing and passing the course.

However, the 27-year-old Lancashire student had found it quite difficult and lonely at first settling down to life in Prishtina, particularly as he had never lived away from home for so long.

For the first year, he lived with an Albanian, who was a professor of French, and his family, and then for the next four years he stayed with another Albanian family and their four children.

It wasn't easy living in Prishtina where temperatures varied from being 40 C to minus 20 C and with the city being in a valley; it meant he had to climb up 124 steps every night to get home. Although the family were hospitable, his only space was his three metres by four metres room, and there were few places to escape to, as the police ordered all the shops, restaurants and cafes to close by 10pm.

He did go to the local cinema occasionally, but his favourite bolthole was the Grand Hotel in the city centre with its plush toilets and comfortable chairs in the lounge. There he could order a coffee and read the English newspapers, sent out by his parents from England, before falling asleep for a couple of hours.

As the post took two weeks to arrive, the papers were out of date, but they still enabled Stephen to keep up to date with his beloved Manchester City football team.

Stephen was determined to learn the language as soon as possible and every day he would go to the university lectures from 7am until noon, then spend an hour in the afternoons evangelising in Albanian to anyone who would listen.

Every Saturday he and Shau Ping, a Chinese student who had also come to Prishtina to learn Albanian, would go to a different town to practise their new language. It was a great encouragement for Stephen that Shau Ping later became a Christian.

As Stephen became more confident with the language, he soon adapted to life in Prishtina, helped by annual trips home and friends and family coming out to see him.

Stephen's journey to Prishtina had really begun in Leigh, Lancashire. Born in Ardwick, Manchester, on May 19, 1959, he went to school in Bolton. As a teenager, Stephen became very keen on football and less keen on having to go to church at Mosley Common as the vicar's son. He was surprised when his brother David came home from university one day and said he had become a Christian and started going to a Christian youth group in Leigh where he had been invited to play in their football team. One night Stephen decided to go along with his brother where he was introduced to the captain of the football team, Philip Butterworth, who was to become a good friend and who also played a part in Stephen's Albanian story.

That summer Stephen became a Christian at a camp near Lulworth Cove in Dorset and on leaving school, he joined the Nat West Bank in 1978.

Five years later when Stephen said he felt called to go to Eastern Europe as a missionary, his father Jack was delighted as he had been all set to go to China as a missionary in 1949, but had been prevented from going by the Communist revolution.

Jack, who had been a European Christian Mission supporter all his life, arranged for his younger son to go to the 1983 ECM Easter conference and meet the leaders, who advised Stephen to join a short-term summer team working in Eastern Europe and then go to theological college. He resigned from the bank and began studying at All Nations College in Ware, Hertfordshire, in September, 1983.

Just before he finished at college, Stephen went to the 1985 ECM Easter conference at Heightside, Rawtenstall. In a room of around 300 people, one of the leaders prophesied: "Somebody in this room has got the call to go to my Albania." The speaker was Sali Rahmani, who became a broadcaster for Trans World Radio and whose programme Captain Berti Dosti had listened to in secret while on duty in the Albanian Army.

A few days later at the conference he had his second confirmation when he switched on his radio to listen to the BBC 8am news and heard that Enver Hoxha had died. He knew then he could go to Albania.

ECM suggested he went to Prishtina, as it was the nearest place to meet Albanians and he could apply to study at the university there. Stephen flew out to meet the principal, Sali Maqedonci, who very amused that Stephen was interested in booking a place there a year in advance and told him to come back in 12 months' time.

"Here in the Balkans," he said, "we tend to leave the registration er... *somewhat later* than you do in England."

Indeed, it was even AFTER the new term had already started that Stephen could eventually register. No problem, the lectures began later still in early October!

Two weeks later Stephen went on a two-week visit to Albania with his friend, Phil Butterworth, from the Leigh youth group. They travelled by coach from Huddersfield on a trip organised by a Yorkshire Communist miners' group, Yorkshire Tours – costing just £228.

Three days and three nights after leaving Huddersfield, and staying in surprisingly luxurious hotels on the way, the party of 28 arrived in Albania on October 4, 1985.

He was shocked at the primitive standards of farming. "I counted up to 500 people, mostly women, working in some fields, toiling in 90-degree temperatures. I did spot some tractors and harvesters, but they were very few."

He said the drab towns were characterised by so many people hanging around and the absence of traffic. The shops were in mostly dilapidated buildings, which were difficult to find as they had neither adverts nor window displays, and had few basic items on sale. Food was very scarce and meat was impossible to find outside the hotel dining rooms.

"I saw one shop selling cookers that were obsolete in Britain years ago," added Stephen, "yet in every town there was a bookshop with stacks of books, mostly the works of Enver Hoxha, on display.

"I was reliably informed that due to a paper shortage and their 'popularity' 95 per cent of them would be recycled unsold, for other uses."

Stephen later found out what that was when he started living in Albania in 1991 – the pages of the Hoxha books were used as toilet paper!

In Durres, the main port and second largest city in Albania, he also saw many people going on their cultural 6pm walkabout as they did in Prishtina. But whereas in Kosovo the streets seemed alive with a bubbling, vibrant populace, the scene in Albania was subdued with the smiles replaced by impassive, sullen faces and the noise replaced by relative silence.

Also, the poverty was obvious with most Albanians looking underfed and wearing simple well-worn outdated clothes. Stephen said he never once saw an Albanian child clutching a toy car or a doll, only bits of wood and metal they had found in the streets.

Vehicles were mainly lorries struggling along the dirt tracks; private cars were banned and the lucky people who owned bicycles had the freedom of the roads.

There were some old Eastern European cars in the capital Tirana, but the official guide admitted that only Party members used them.

Stephen said they visited many places, passing thousands and thousands of military pillboxes.

"Everywhere there were signs declaring the praises of the dead leader Enver Hoxha, yet there didn't seem all that much to shout about," said Stephen.

On a visit to a noisy and smelly factory he said the looms and other machinery were dilapidated with few safety devices.

"We were also told by the supervisor that the workforce worked round the clock to maximise output," he added. "But I heard a conflicting report that many factories were now on a two-day week, due to lack of electricity, and the workers had been laid off unpaid."

On a visit to a kindergarten the 3-6-year-old boys and girls all trooped out in single file, stamping their feet, saluting with clenched fist and shouting Enver Hoxha! Enver Hoxha!

One day they passed a wedding procession where the bridegroom and his new bride were slowly walking along the country road, accompanied by an accordionist, violinist and singers and a crowd of 80 or so guests dancing around them. "It was heart warming to see a little happiness in this bleak country," said Stephen.

What the Yorkshire left wing miners thought of Stephen and Phil, who were so different in education, background and outlook, they never found out. However, they did discover one day what one of the others thought.

An English journalist, who had gone incognito to write a travel report for a national British newspaper, suddenly asked them: "Are you real? You're Christians, aren't you?"

"What do you mean?" replied Stephen.

"I've been watching you two. You don't swear, you don't smoke, you don't get drunk, you don't chase the girls, you're too nice."

They thought it was too dangerous then to admit publicly they were Christians. However, they continued to talk to their two tour guides, Andre and Anton, who wanted to practise their English and, as single men, they were desperate to leave Albania.

Interestingly, Andre later became a Christian and helped translate messages for the Words of Hope programme on Radio 7 in Tirana, a radio station where Berti was later to broadcast from every Monday.

Before leaving Durres for the long coach ride back home to Huddersfield, the tour party challenged the locals to a beach game of football with Albania beating England 2-0.

When Stephen returned home, he was relieved to read the journalist's report in a Sunday paper about the Albanian trip and to find there was no mention of himself nor his friend Phil.

That trip convinced Stephen to return to Prishtina a year later to enrol at the university. He flew out for a two-week language course at Prishtina and was the only English person. Stephen couldn't believe the Kosovans' generosity with meals, accommodation in a student dormitory and education with five hours of Albanian every day, all for free. In the afternoon, they were taken to historical Kosovan sites – also for free.

The day after the course finished, Stephen began life on his own with his Albanian phrasebook, a little knowledge of Albanian and a place in the queue to enrol at Prishtina University.

But he couldn't understand what the enrolling officer was saying to him. As he looked round wondering what to do next a young Kosovo Albanian, Gani Smolica, who was next in the queue and who would later become a key person in Berti's story, said to him in a perfect Oxford English accent: "Excuse me, can I help you?"

Gani really shouldn't have been in that queue to enrol at Prishtina University that day. He was, in fact, a professor who by day taught young medical students and during the evening translated for TV and radio companies to earn some extra money.

He was there because his wife, Adile, another Kosovo Albanian, needed to take a university exam and she thought it was easier for her husband to sort out the paperwork.

Gani was born on September 25, 1958, in the beautiful town of Peja, which is the gateway to Montenegro and famous for being the home of the Serbian Orthodox Church.

When Gani was 12, the family moved to Prishtina. He went to Prishtina University in 1977 where he met two people who were to have a big influence on his life.

Firstly in 1976, he was introduced to a young student Adile who went to the same group of lectures to study English language and literature. They became friends and five years later in 1981, Gani and Adile were married. By the time, they met Stephen they already had two daughters Besiana and Doruntina and were later to have two sons, Lorik and Shpetim.

Secondly, in 1986, after Gani helped Stephen enrol at university they used to meet for Coca Cola and kebabs where they would help each other improve their English and their Albanian. When Gani became a Christian in December 1988, Stephen and the church pastor baptised him.

"I did notice a difference," said Adile, "Gani became a better husband and he started looking after the children more and helping around the house." Then Adile too became a believer in March 1989.

That chance meeting between Stephen and Gani at Prishtina University was the start of a lifelong friendship and as Stephen said: "We both changed each other's lives."

8

A HIGH POINT – AND A LOW POINT

Although Enver Hoxha had died in 1985, nothing really changed in Albania for the next four years. His chosen successor, Ramiz Alia, who was the leader of the Party of Labour, the Communist Party, continued with the one-party state and using the army to keep order.

Despite becoming an officer when he was older than many of his colleagues, Berti's military record and expertise were not in question. He proved that when he was the star soldier during a big military exercise in Kavaja in 1986. Every kind of weapon was on show and Berti's skills were rated as first class, particularly as he had introduced new ideas and ways of using radio communications.

The top brass in the Albanian army noticed Berti's abilities and the exercise was such a success that he was presented with the Urdhri i Sherbimit Ushtarak te Klasit III, the third highest military medal in the country, on July 8, 1986. The citation said the medal was for "distinguished work in organisation and leadership in the military base where he served and attaining very high achievements of practice with his fellow soldiers."

The medal was signed by the top general, the 1st secretary of the Albanian Army and was presented at the Kavaja army HQ in the presence of officers only.

It was a tremendous achievement for someone who had been an officer for only three years and who was not yet 30 years old.

His father must have been proud of his son who had eclipsed his military record and that of Berti's brother Iliri. However, unlike the British army, such honours are not presented with pomp and ceremony in front of family members. In those days, the army was a very secret and closed place, even to Albanians. If any Albanian, who was not a full-time soldier, stumbled across a military location, he or she could be arrested and accused of spying. Even Berti's father, who had now retired from the military, was not allowed inside the base.

Nevertheless, although Berti's military record was impeccable, he was about to blot his party biography again.

He decided that if he was to get promotion, he needed to become a member of the Party, which with his background should have been a formality.

Only the best could become Party members and after requesting to join, officials then investigated very carefully every aspect of the person and his or her family.

They would go back to the third and fourth generations and see how devoted they and their family were to the Party.

If a person had long hair or the fashionable drainpipe trousers, then that person had been tempted by foreign influences.

If they were well educated, smartly dressed and knew another language, they were labelled foreign intellectuals, which would count against them.

If they showed an interest in world news or TV or foreign films, that could also be minus points to their name.

Everyone watched everyone else in Albania. There were a web of spies and people would sell information, real or invented, to the authorities.

Berti waited for the Party to tell him he had been successful.

He knew members were called to a prestigious ceremony in the The Party's Meeting Room, a hall where there were the Secretary of the Party, other VIPs and a podium at the front where all loyal Party members were seated.

The candidate was kept outside while his or her proposer addressed the Party members and put the case for the person to be admitted to the Party. The irony was that the officials were too afraid to reject anyone, in case it reflected badly on them and their career.

Then the person was called into the room where he or she said what an honour it was and promised that they would work day and night for the Party. They swore they would be ready to give their life for the sake of the Party and that they would be "first in sacrificing and last in pretending". They would also be prepared to work anywhere in the country.

If the officials suspected he or she had any intellectual leanings, they would be sent out into the country and given a lowly-paid job there.

However, Berti thought he would be protected from all that with his military background.

By now, Berti had his own office at the base, the only one who did, and it contained the treasured possession of a black and white TV. In Albania permission was needed to buy a TV as their number were limited, and only those of good standing could have one. It was the same with going to university, getting a job or a house; people needed a good biography and Party approval. Those who didn't have a 'clean biography' ended up squashed into a one-roomed house with no luxuries.

One evening it had been a long, 24-hour shift and as usual, nothing had happened. The airwaves were quiet; the base was deserted as there was only Berti and a guard duty soldier working. He was feeling tired, it was 1am, and he thought he would switch on the TV. He started to watch Boot Hill, a cowboy film – but he could understand only a little as it was in Italian.

Suddenly, two officials quietly came into the office without knocking – the Kommissar and the base Commandant.

Berti was accused of two mistakes, firstly watching a foreign TV station and secondly of not doing his duty. Although he wasn't asleep, he hadn't been walking around the base to check on the soldier on guard duty. If he had, he would have found, just as the Kommissar and Commandant had, that there was no one guarding the base. What Berti didn't realise was that the soldier was in the shadows outside his office, quietly watching the same film with him through a window.

The next day Berti was told he was going to be fined for his early morning misdemeanours. Although he had not committed a huge mistake, he was so bitter and angry that he didn't go in to work for three days. Then when he returned to the Suzoltaj base one of his friends, an officer, said: "What have you done wrong? I have heard your name mentioned in discussions a lot. You were close to being accepted to becoming a Party member, but now you are going to be rejected."

Although it was a bad offence to be criticised at the base, it was far more serious when it went to the Party.

Berti was so furious he went to see the Kommissar and challenged him: "Why did you tell the Party, and why haven't you told me they have rejected me from becoming a member?"

The Kommissar replied: "It was my duty to tell the truth to the Party."

"But it wasn't that serious an offence," retorted Berti.

"It is my duty to inform the Party of everything," he replied.

With that the conversation ended. The duty soldier received just a criticism while Berti never did hear officially that the Party had rejected him.

A while later Berti remembered the television incident as he thought about what he had heard on the radio while he was twiddling the dials.

"If you want to find out more about God we will meet again tomorrow," said the presenter, one night in late 1989.

Berti was intrigued; but dare he take the chance? It was bad enough to be caught watching a cowboy film in Italian, but to be found listening to a Christian radio programme would be a second, and far more serious, offence. God was never mentioned while he was at school, so why should a 15-minute programme from the enemy in the West intrigue him? To this day, he doesn't know why, although "something deep down was telling me to listen." He added: "Religion was a total mystery, but I wanted to find out more, particularly about creation."

Berti knew the risks of being caught, losing his job and the effect on his family, especially as by now Berti and Tatjana had a second child, a son Dorian, born on April 23, 1988. So, he decided to talk to Tatjana about the idea.

"I was worried," she admitted, "but I have always supported Berti and knew he would be very careful."

Berti thought it was a risk worth taking, and remembering what had happened in the TV incident, he used his military brain to reduce as many of the dangers as possible.

He knew the programme came on at 8.45pm when he would again be alone in the base with just a soldier on guard duty.

Firstly, he checked the soldier was on duty at the entrance to the base and told him to phone through immediately if there were any visitors.

Then he walked into his office, which was only about 10ft by 10ft and was full of radios, and carefully shut the door. At least he would hear anyone coming into his office this time.

He went to his desk, put on his headphones, and settled back to tune in to Trans World Radio. With the TV, there was no remote control so he could not change channels easily if someone walked in. However, with the radio, he could move the dial easily. Even better if someone did see him with his headphones on, as he did most of the day when he was on duty, they would presume he was doing his job of protecting Albania's defences from a surprise attack.

The programme asked 'Who is God?' a question Berti had never considered before. The presenter finished by saying: If you want to find out more, write to me, Luan Mateu at PO Box 349, Monte Carlo, Monaco.

However, it was a while before Berti would pluck up courage and write to the radio station.

What he didn't know then and would find out much later was that the address was a postbox for Trans World Radio and Luan Mateu was a nom-de-plume. He was, in fact, Sali Rahmani, an Albanian born in Kosovo, who was now recording the programmes in England where he worked for the European Christian Mission, an organisation that had already influenced Stephen Bell.

So how did Trans World Radio end up broadcasting into atheistic and communist Albania from capitalistic and democratic Monaco? That story begins when an American arrived in Spain in 1948.

9

MONTE CARLO – AND NEARLY BUST

Spain was the last place on earth American Paul E. Freed wanted to be on that muggy day in 1948. The 30-year-old had been persuaded to go to the International Youth for Christ Conference in Beatenberg, Switzerland, where two zealous Spaniards invited him back to Barcelona for a short visit to discuss how they could reach 30,000,000 people with the gospel in the second most mountainous country in Europe. The more Paul thought about it, the more he realised radio was the only answer. "But I did not have a dime of support," he said.[12]

Paul, whose parents were missionaries in southern Syria, was educated in Jerusalem and Beirut before

---

12 *Towers to Eternity* by Dr. Paul E. Freed, published by Trans World Radio.

he returned to America to go to Wheaton College, Illinois and Nyack Missionary Training Institute, New York, where his father had enrolled almost 20 years earlier.

In 1948, he became Youth for Christ director in Greensboro, North Carolina, and it was there the movement's founder, Torrey Johnson, persuaded him to go to the conference in Switzerland, which ended with the detour to Spain.

When he returned from Spain he resigned from Youth for Christ, became an evangelist and set up a business designing and building trailers and homes, which he thought, could become a good financial basis to realise his radio dream.

It wasn't until 1951 that Paul took his wife Betty Jane to Spain for the first time, where a Spanish interpreter told them: "You ought to go over to Tangier, that's the best place for broadcasting."

The next day they went to Morocco to visit an 80-year-old English missionary, Mr Elson, who owned land and a small cottage.

When Paul suggested to him about the possibility of giving the old mission property for his proposed Gospel radio studio, and living accommodation, he replied: "Young man, if you can give your life for mission, the least I can do is give my property."

Mr Elson discussed it with his relatives and they agreed a compromise price of 15,000 dollars, way below its real value. Paul and Betty now knew they could start a radio station and its address would be Tangier, but how could they get the support of American Christians?

Paul and Betty Jane returned to the USA and produced a film, Banderilla, about the project. For two and a half months the couple, now with two young children, went on an 11,000-mile deputation trip. They got plenty of support but little money for the radio station. Nevertheless, on February 11, 1952, they founded Trans World Radio, under the name International Evangelism – the same day as their third child, Donna Jean, was born. But, how were they going to run the station?

Critics were quick to point out it didn't exist yet, there was no board of directors, no long-term plan, it wasn't linked to an official missionary group and anyway, why start yet another radio station?

Despite the opposition, the Freeds, with their three children under five years old, decided to sell their house and return to Tangier.

Paul's first job was to get the necessary government permit to build the station.

As he was walking through the noisy streets of Tangier an American stopped him and said: "My name is Southworth. I understand you are trying to build a radio station." Paul knew Mr Southworth had his own station in the international zone of Tangier as he continued: "I'd like to suggest that your station be put up under my permit. You may save a year or more in time."

Paul was reluctant at first, but later agreed it was a perfect solution. Mr Southworth would build the transmitters and antennae and then lease the whole package back to them. He had the permit, the land and the engineering crew, and it would involve a much smaller cash outlay for the Freeds.

But what about the money needed to buy the nearby beautiful property overlooking the Straits of Gibraltar, which would be ideal for a separate radio studio and flats for the staff to live in? How would they raise the 15,000 dollars?

By chance when they had returned to the States for a holiday, they met up with a friend, Clarence Staats. They mentioned the property overlooking the Straits of Gibraltar and the price to him. "I don't see why we can't arrange that for you," he said, and later mailed the whole amount to Tangier.

Finally, "The Voice of Tangier", as it came to be known, went on the air in 1954 with a budget of 10,000 dollars for the first year. Ten years later that figure had increased by more than 100 times that amount.

For the next five years, it was tough finding money to run the station as interest in Christian radio was almost non-existent among evangelicals in Europe, and it was just as difficult finding staff to produce the programmes.

However, the Freeds persevered and the work continued to grow. In 1956, the old transmitter was replaced so they were able to broadcast to 24 different language groups, beaming specific programmes into almost every country in Europe, North Africa and the Middle East.

Then disaster struck. In April 1959, the Moroccan government announced that every radio station in the country was to be nationalised by the end of the year. So that was the end of broadcasting from Morocco.

At least The Voice of Tangier did have another option. Two years earlier, they were looking to expand when Paul's mother said to him just six months before she died in November 1957, that he should look at Monte Carlo.

Despite what seemed a strange choice to relocate to probably the wealthiest piece of land in Europe, Paul switched his New York flight the next morning in spring 1957 and headed to Monte Carlo instead. The talks with Radio Monte Carlo executive Erik Bosio, on top of the mountain by the antennae that had been put up by Hitler's regime during the war to spread the Nazi propaganda went well, but nothing was agreed.

Paul decided that he would offer the Radio Monte Carlo board of directors an advance of 50,000 American dollars towards installing the extra antennae system and the 100,000-watt transmitter for The Voice of Tangier.

But then Erik Bosio told him the board now wanted the total payment of 500,000 American dollars in advance and this would be the only opportunity. Also, the board would not be interested in investing any of its own funds in the project.

If agreed, the money was to be paid in six instalments, the first when they approved the project and the other five within a year of all the equipment being put up. If any of the instalments were late, the whole project would collapse.

"Even the one-sixth figure for the down payment of 83,000 dollars sounded fantastic," recalled Paul. "I honestly wondered if I had lost my mind."

The board agreed the price and said Paul could lease the radio facility full-time for ten years with an indefinite number of renewals. The next problem was where to find the money as there was only a month between drawing up the contract in August 1959 and the next Radio Monte Carlo board meeting in September.

Two years earlier in the autumn of 1957 when his mother caught pneumonia, and was bored in a London hospital, she decided to try to tune in to The Voice of Tangier. She called about 20 people over to listen, including a Norwegian visitor. Later, he invited Paul to meet him and his Haanes family in Norway where he found they owned a large shipping company and several other successful businesses.

On the day of the September board meeting, when the first payment was due, a cheque for Paul arrived from the Haanes family for 83,000 dollars. However, there were still five more payments needed.

When it came to the second payment, they were still 8,000 dollars short on the final day.

At 11.30am, Paul said to his team: "I'll have to leave for the bank now or else I won't make the deadline."

As he neared the bank one of the workers walking down the street waved him over saying he had just picked up a letter at the post office with a cheque for 5,000 dollars in it.

Paul was encouraged, but when he met the bank president he had to tell him they were still 3,000 dollars short.

As they went into the president's office, the phone rang. The president almost dropped the phone. "How in the world can this happen?"

"Well, who was it?" stammered Paul.

He said a telegram had come from Western Union wiring funds to the account of Trans World Radio for 3,000 dollars adding: "I sure wish I knew who sent it."

An amazed Paul said quietly: "Well, I know who sent it. God sent it."

"Who did you say?" The president leaned over the desk towards him.

Still shaking his head, Paul repeated his comment: "God sent it."

"I didn't quite hear you. What was the man's name?" asked the bank official.

This time Paul turned to him, and repeated slowly and deliberately: "Almighty God sent it."

Now the banker shook his head. He said almost inaudibly: "You know, I believe, you're right."

Money then came into the radio station for the next three instalments, but there was still one more bank drama to go before the final payment for the Monte Carlo station was complete.

The afternoon before the final deadline day, they were 1,500 dollars short.

The next morning at Barclay's Bank, an official told Paul: "No other funds have come in since yesterday. But if you don't mind, I'd like to take a few minutes to refigure it.

He returned with a mysterious smile: "You made it".

"What do you mean, we made it," asked Paul.

"You'll never believe it," he said, "but the value of the German mark has jumped in value since we figured the total, which adds exactly 1,500 dollars to your account."

On October 16, 1960, the Voice of Tangier became Trans World Radio and went on the air, 13 months since they signed the contract with Radio Monte Carlo in September 1959.

The station broadcasts in 24 different languages using nationals to record in their own country and send their tapes to Monte Carlo for transmission.

However, all this stress had had an effect on Paul's health. Nine months later in June 1961, he returned to the States for a holiday and while playing tennis he had a serious heart attack at the age of 42 years old and nearly died.

During the first year in Monte Carlo 18,000 letters arrived at the radio. Then the station was granted permission to use Radio Monte Carlo's giant 400,000-watt medium wave (standard broadcast) AM transmitter after 10pm, so they could reach many homes in the heart of Europe during prime evening hours.

The number of broadcasts has continued to expand so today Trans World Radio reaches more than 190 countries in more than 200 languages and dialects. In the 1960s, 70s, 80s and early 90s more and more letters flowed in from every country, apart from Albania. They hadn't had a single letter in reply to the Albania programme, since they had started broadcasting there in 1968. Trans World Radio officials, and particularly the presenter of the programme, the Albanian-Kosovan, Sali Rahmani, must have wondered whether anyone in Albania was listening. But how did Sali end up sending the programme into his home country?

10

ONCE I WAS BLIND, BUT NOW I CAN SEE

For the first two years of his life Kosovo Albanian Sali Rahmani couldn't see a thing. Most of his Muslim family thought he would be blind for life but his mother, Hanumsha, didn't lose hope that one day he would be able to see.

She realised as soon as Sali was born on April 14, 1946, in Ferizaj in south eastern Kosovo, that there was something wrong with his eyes, which didn't seem to respond to movement or noise. She took him to Skopje Hospital and they twice operated on his eyes without success. Hanumsha knew one of the leading eye experts who lived in Greece, so she sold some of their household goods to pay for the trip to Thessalonica, but even he couldn't restore Sali's sight.

However, she still believed that her son would be healed. So, every August she left her husband Hasan and family in Ferizaj to go to a Catholic shrine in nearby Letnica for three weeks.

She joined thousands of pilgrims from Croatia, Albania, Serbia and Kosovo at the huge white church with two bell towers on a hill dominating the town. Hanumsha believed that if she prayed before the church's rare black Madonna statue her son would be healed.

When Sali was two and a half she took him with her to the shrine for his first time. As he walked round the church on the first day, he suddenly pointed with his finger at the famous picture of Jesus the Lamb behind the altar and said: "Look, Mama."

Hanumsha couldn't believe it, her son had never pointed at anything in his life before.

"Do you see something?" she asked nervously. "Yes," said Sali. She tested him again, asking him to look at other things in the church before being convinced he could now see.

A couple of days later they returned home for a huge family celebration, where even his father, Hasan, a dedicated Communist who was very anti religion, had to accept something had happened to his son.

Sali went with his mother every year on the pilgrimage until he was 13, because she was worried that his blindness would return.

The doctors couldn't explain what had happened to Sali, except to say he had had serious complications in both eyes as well as cataracts. Afterwards, Hanumsha gave birth to four other children, three sons and a daughter, and they were all born with perfect sight.

Sali wasn't the only pilgrim who had been affected by a visit to the church in Letnica.

A young girl, Agnes Bojaxhiu, born on August 26, 1910, near Skopje, was a regular pilgrim there. She enjoyed the choir's singing, and went on several retreats at the church. At the age of 17, the same year her father, an activist in the Albanian nationalist movement, was poisoned in the civil war with Yugoslavia, she dedicated herself to helping the world's poor and hungry. She became a nun, joined the Order of the Loreto sisters and taught for many years in Calcutta, India, where she was better known as Mother Theresa. In 1946, she founded the Missionaries of Charity, just two years after Enver Hoxha took control of Albania.

Ironically, while this Kosovo Albanian Mother Theresa was becoming one of the most famous Christians in the world, another Albanian, Enver Hoxha, was banning religion, declaring in 1967 that there was no God and stating that his country was the world's first atheist state.

Mother Theresa outlived Hoxha and when Albania began to open its borders in 1989, she visited her homeland and a branch of her Missionaries of Charity was established there a year later. She died in Calcutta in 1997 and was given a state funeral, attended by more than 12,000 mourners.

Sali and his two younger brothers had had a reasonable standard of living in a better than average house as his father was a police officer. Unlike Albania, President Tito allowed religion to continue in Yugoslavia, including Kosovo.

Sali went to the local school, Tefik Çanga, from the age of six until 16. It brought back many poignant memories for his father. During the war, his father had been a double agent. By day, he had been a police officer working for the Germans, by night he worked for the Partisans, the resistance movement. The Germans believed he had infiltrated the Partisans to provide them with information, while he gave the Partisans intelligence about the German invaders. His best friend, Tefik Çanga, also worked as a spy, but he was arrested. The Germans hung him by his feet outside the school in the square and forced the town people to watch him die. However, they never forgot the bravery of their local hero, Tefik Çanga, and named the school after him.

Later, Sali went to college to study economics and accountancy – and to form a pop group. In England it was the era of the Beatles, the Rolling Stones and their records were as popular in Kosovo as in the rest of the world. As he could play the guitar, Sali spent the evening singing in his group, which he called The Illyrians, the Roman name for Albania. During the day, he studied and after qualifying he worked in the accounts department at a furniture factory while in the evening, he played in the band with three others.

Sali was bass guitar and soloist, the drummer was a Serbian, while two of Sali's cousins were lead guitarist and guitarist. They were going to be called the Blue Stars and each had a blue star tattoo on their arm, which Sali still has today, but they decided instead to go for The Illyrians and wore Beatles T-shirts.

When the young accountant got bored with his furniture factory job, he decided in the spring of 1972 to seek fame and fortune in Australia, which meant first attending an interview at their nearest embassy, which was in Vienna, Austria.

He set off on the 1,000-kilometre journey with little money and just one set of clothes, a pair of white trousers and a flowery silk shirt.

There in Austria's capital 24-year-old Sali found romance and God, in that order.

At the Australian Embassy he was about to be ushered back on to the streets when he produced an official letter from the Ambassador. By chance, the Ambassador's wife was in the office and she took pity on the young Kosovan, as she had also been born in Yugoslavia, in nearby Bosnia.

When she learnt he had nowhere to stay she offered him the spare room at their house "for a couple of days".

"I couldn't believe it," said Sali. "Here I was a poor Kosovan, eating in the ambassador's house and mixing with posh people."

As his stay became more permanent so did his friendship with the Ambassador's daughter. They started planning to get married, to go to Australia and to run a chicken business just outside Canberra, which her family owned.

Soon after the wedding discussions, Sali was walking through Vienna when he came across an open-air Christian meeting in the Prater. As one of the city's most famous landmarks with a funfair and a big wheel, it gained a reputation as the place to meet, where lovers came on secret dates, where great composers performed and where poets and writers found inspiration. It was also where the increasing number of illegal immigrants, who had escaped from Communist countries behind the Iron Curtain, such as Russia, East Germany, Poland, Hungary, Romania. Bulgaria, Czechoslovakia and Yugoslavia, met.

International Christians decided to try to help these people, and they started an hour-long Sunday afternoon open-air service there in English, German and Serbo-Croat.

Sali was intrigued to hear songs in Serbo-Croat, a language he recognised, so he went over and met Barbara Jamieson, a worker with ECM, who invited him to go to church.

It was amazing that Barbara had ended up in Vienna doing street evangelism, as she was a qualified nurse and midwife. Born in Bridlington, East Yorkshire, in 1934 her father, John, a fisherman decided it was safer to move to the Shetland Islands when the Second World War broke out in 1939. He was right, a few months after they left a German bomb landed on their house in Bridlington and badly damaged it.

After being converted at a Billy Graham rally and then training as a nurse Barbara later joined ECM, eventually going to Vienna.

Sali turned up at the recently-formed evangelical church the following Sunday where he was amazed to hear the pastor, Misko Horvatek, talking about how Jesus had healed the blind man, Bartimaeus. After the service, he was even more surprised when he went to the back of the church and flicked open a St John's Gospel. There on the first page was a picture of Jesus and the lamb. It was the same one he had seen when he was a two-and-a-half-year-old boy behind the altar at Letnica.

A few weeks later, he went to talk to the pastor who said: "Do you believe in Jesus, the Son of God, who was born of the Virgin Mary?"

Sali nodded. The pastor then asked: "Do you believe Jesus came to earth doing good and healing people?"

Again, Sali said yes, and so he asked a third question: "Do you believe Jesus died on the cross for you?" Sali nodded and that evening, August 14, 1972, Sali went to the pastor's house where he prayed with him, the pastor's wife and their three children.

"I had been healed of my own blindness, now I was healed of my spiritual blindness," said Sali. "I now had an overwhelming peace in my life."

He wasn't the only one to feel different – his girlfriend did as well. Instead of emigrating he wanted to stay with his new church friends in Vienna – and to this day he has never been to Australia. His girlfriend said they would have to say goodbye. Sali then had the difficult job of going to the embassy to see the official who was overseeing his emigration papers to ask him to withdraw his application for Australia. That official was the ambassador, who nearly became Sali's father-in-law.

It wasn't only the end of a relationship, but of his six months of free board and lodging in the ambassador's house.

Sali's own father, Hasan, also took a dim view of his son's news at becoming a Christian. Don't ever bother coming home, was his reply. Sali began writing to his parents regularly, although for a long time he never heard anything back.

Then two years later Sali was walking through Vienna when a man, who looked just like his father, walked past him. Sali looked again and to his amazement realised it was.

"Daddy, it's me," he shouted.

His father turned and said: "I was looking for a person in black garments and a beard."

He thought his son had become an Orthodox priest and had travelled the 1,000-kilometre journey to check that he was all right.

Although it wasn't an emotional reunion, they enjoyed a couple of days together before his father returned to Kosovo without saying anything about the future.

Next time he went to church the pastor said he had been given a message from Sali's father that said: "You can tell my son he can come home now."

Sali, who still had hardly any clothes, had managed to find a bed in a hostel. He heard that a steel components factory was looking for workers, so he put on his white trousers and silk flowered shirt and went to meet the manager, who told him to report next day at 9am. The manager, who was surprised to see him arrive in the same white trousers and silk flowered shirt, said he was now a cleaner. It wasn't many minutes before his precious white trousers turned black in the steel works, but at least Sali was earning so he could afford to buy some new clothes.

The manager was impressed by Sali's work commitment and it wasn't long before he trained him up to be an engineering worker, which meant he doubled his salary overnight.

His new-found wealth coincided with the time the church was looking for a new car. Sali had always wanted his own car and he thought the obvious solution was to buy one and let the church use it when he didn't need it. He went to the local garage and there saw the car of his dreams. Even though he hadn't yet passed his driving test he proudly drove it home to show his friend Branko Tihojevic, who was teaching him to drive, and also his pastor Misko, what he had bought.

They couldn't believe their eyes. "We can't have that car, you will have to take it back immediately," spluttered Misko.

Sali had bought a bright red Ford Mustang, a huge American car, which he had seen Elvis Presley drive in the Viva Las Vegas film.

They took Sali back to the garage and Misko explained the problem to a bemused car salesman. They returned with a much smaller and a much more sober coloured Ford car.

But Sali continued to like flashy cars. When a few months later an Australian volunteer with the European Christian Mission offered to drive him home to see his family for a few days, he couldn't resist being driven in an open top red MG.

However, Sali soon had second thoughts as they sped south; twice the police stopped them for speeding.

News about Sali coming home spread through his family and friends and they all wanted to meet him having heard he had changed. Sali certainly made an entrance arriving at his family home in a red sports car.

Dozens crowded into the family home to talk to him and many didn't leave until 3am including the local priest who said accusingly: "You have changed religion."

"No," replied Sali, "religion has changed me."

When Sali returned to Vienna there was a letter waiting for him from the Billy Graham organisation inviting him to a convention in Geneva.

"Why are they inviting me? I don't speak English, I would be wasting my time," he complained to his pastor.

"Perhaps they invited you because you are the only Albanian believer they know," he replied.

Why don't the Albanian people know God, he wondered? Suddenly he realised that perhaps God was calling him to serve his people in Albania. But how could he go there, it was a closed country even to him as a Kosovo Albanian?

Then he remembered the story of the paralysed man in the Bible (Luke chapter 5 verses 17-39). There his four friends could not see Jesus because of the crowds blocking the door. So, they went up the outside steps and let him in from above through the roof.

If Sali couldn't get into Albania by land because the doors were shut, why not go in from above – with radio messages. But how could he do that?

By now, Sali and his friend Branko were fully involved with helping the European Christian Mission workers at the church. One day the ECM staff asked Sali and Branko if they would like to go to Bible college in Britain sponsored by the mission. They would spend the first year at the ECM HQ in Heightside, Rawtenstall, and then go to the Lebanon Bible College in Berwick-upon-Tweed.

They jumped at the chance and just before Sali left Vienna, he was asked to take a dozen radio scripts to ECM, written by a Yugoslav Christian in Peja, Simo Ralevic.

Three important events happened the day Sali arrived in England on Wednesday, November 14, 1973.

Firstly, the whole country was celebrating as HRH Princess Anne married Captain Mark Phillips; secondly, it was Sali's first visit to England and thirdly and sadly, it was the day Alfred Andoni, who had helped send radio programmes into Albania, died.

When in 1967 Albania declared itself an atheistic country ECM general director, the Rev Stuart Harris, was praying for a way to get the Christian message into Albania by radio. ECM already had a radio studio because they were recording messages for their work in Italy, but he needed someone who could speak Albanian and who lived in England.

In July 1968, Stuart heard the BBC World Service was cutting back on its foreign services, including Alfred Andoni's job on the Albania desk. Alfred was an Albanian, married to an English woman who lived in London.

He had an interesting CV. During the day he worked for the BBC on their Albanian broadcasts. In the evening he listened to Albanian radio to gather information about what was going on inside the closed country and to report back to his new masters, British Intelligence.

On top of that Stuart offered to pay Alfred to translate messages from English into Albanian, which were sent from a Christian radio studio in south London to ECM's Heightside where a technical expert forwarded them to Monte Carlo to beam into Albania.

The first time they went to record the programme, the Christians said: "We will start with a prayer."

"Why," asked Alfred? Five years later, just before he died, Alfred asked to meet Stuart in London and said he now wanted to become a believer.

It was probably the first time a radio presenter had been converted by his own programme.

When Alfred died, the radio staff were wondering where they were going to find another Albanian speaker for the programme when in walked Sali – complete with 12 Albanian radio scripts.

Over the next few months Sali translated other scripts written by ECM staff for the programme before on Easter Sunday, 1974, he wrote and broadcast his own message.

For the next 21 years, Sali faithfully broadcast the Christian message, which were a mixture of Bible readings and studies, children's Bible stories and practical Christian teaching, including how to hold Communion services in secret.

He used a nom de plume, Luan Mateu, to protect his identity and because the name would appeal to all Albanians, as Luan was a Muslim name, and Mateu a Roman Catholic one.

Little did Sali know then that there were many people listening secretly in Albania, including a top government official, army officer Berti, and many adults and children, so justifying the faith of the radio staff, and particularly Dr Paul Freed, who had set up Trans World Radio all those years ago.

But at least Sali knew he had one listener in Kosovo. One of his biggest fans was his dad who told everyone in their town, Ferizaj: "Listen to my son; he is speaking on the radio from England."

His father and one of Sali's brothers were so enthusiastic that they gave out many posters about the programme.

However, some were handed to the local police. That was to have serious repercussions for Sali when he returned home a few years later.

11

WE KNOW YOU ARE A CIA SPY

Sali had enjoyed his two years while at Bible college in Berwick-upon-Tweed, but one question was troubling him. Should he marry a college girl he had become very friendly with, Helen McGinley, a Glaswegian Christian? She was very involved with Bible Centred Ministries International, a group dedicated to reaching children and developing churches worldwide, and she might soon go abroad and he would never see her again. But Sali didn't know what he would be doing when he finished college.

When ECM invited Sali to move to Munich to work alongside another of their workers, Tom Lewis, he decided to accept that offer and ask Helen to marry him.

On June 26, 1976, which would later turn out to be a very auspicious date, they were married at Mosspark Baptist Church in Glasgow.

For the next four years, Sali threw himself into his work with overseas workers, while he continued to send his Christian tapes back to ECM, Rawtenstall, to be sent into Albania via Monte Carlo.

At first, he produced one programme a week, then it grew to two and finally three nights a week. When an American donated £40,000, Trans World Radio was later able to broadcast seven nights a week.

Sali lived in a block of flats and he recorded the programmes in the bedroom. However, he would try to work when the lift wasn't being used, as it was so noisy that it could be heard on his tapes.

Every Friday afternoon Sali used to go down to Munich railway station. The 5.17 train to Thessalonica was when Yugoslavs and Kosovo Albanians would return home and Sali was given permission by the railway authorities to preach in the station foyer, to give out free literature and to sell Bibles.

Sali went there every Friday without any problems. Then one day, while he was preaching, he noticed two well-built men in suits watching him suspiciously. He thought nothing more about it and continued giving his Christian message. As he finished and turned his back, the two men suddenly grabbed him and frogmarched him to a nearby toilet cubicle. "You are in big trouble," one of them said to him.

"I was so shocked I couldn't say anything at first," said Sali. "What the two didn't realise was that as they spoke in Serbo-Croatian, I could understand everything they were saying."

He realised that they were planning to drug him and then take him back secretly to Yugoslavia. As he was dragged into the toilet, he saw a German police officer and managed to shout for help in German.

As the police officer came over, the two abductors let go of Sali and melted into the crowd.

Sali was shaken by this incident. However, as the weeks went by, he forgot about it, and settled back into family and church life.

Their first daughter was born and she was named Hanumsha after her grandmother. Later Sali and Helen had two sons, Simon and Luan, the latter after his radio nom de plume.

In 1980, they left Munich and moved to Vienna to work in the ECM offices where Sali continued with his radio broadcasting, but all the time the question continued to nag him: Was anyone listening?

In April 1983, he decided to combine a trip home to Kosovo to see his parents and to go into the nearby villages and towns to find if there were any listeners to his programme there.

Although ECM weren't too keen on the idea, Sali persuaded them to let him go, and he and a radio operator and technician, Peter Harrison, set off for Ferizaj, Kosovo, in a rusty old Renault. Peter had joined ECM in January 1970 and he prepared the tapes to send to Trans World Radio so they could beam Sali's message into Albania.

Everything went well until Peter and Sali came to the Slovenian border. They were searched thoroughly; their shoes were X-rayed plus their vehicle was stripped with even the wheels taken off and examined. "Afterwards, they put the car over a pit and checked the underneath, with them pointing out things that the Austrian mechanics had missed in the MOT inspection," recalled Peter.

Sali told Peter to return to Vienna and he would make his own way to Ferizaj, but Peter refused, knowing that as he was a British passport holder, the authorities would think twice about doing anything to Sali.

The customs officials treated Peter very politely, but told Sali not to tell Peter anything. However, Sali replied: "He is my friend." This worried them because in Albanian culture there is always a strong bond between friends.

Sali, as a Yugoslav national, bore the brunt of the questions. He was interrogated in a room on his own at the customs post for five hours and had his passport taken off him.

They asked him: "What are you doing in Vienna? Who are you working for? Why are you forcibly propagating the Christian gospel?"

Sali patiently explained he was a missionary and all he was doing was presenting the Christian message. Then they asked him: Why are you working for Radio Free Europe?

This was an American radio station, which had broadcast from Munich to Russia and Eastern Europe during the Cold War to counteract the Communist propaganda. Up until 1972, the American spy network, the Central Intelligence Agency, had funded it and the Russians had tried unsuccessfully to jam the broadcasts.

While in Munich, Sali lived very close to the Radio Free Europe studios and he had been invited to do some broadcasting. He was tempted, but after talking it through with ECM, he decided against it.

Now he confidently told the officials that they were wrong, he had never worked for Radio Free Europe.

After five hours of questioning and checking documents, Sali and Peter were allowed to continue to Ferizaj. However, there was one condition – Sali would have to stay at his parents' house for the whole month and the police would call for him every day and escort him to the police station. They had wanted to keep Sali in a police station cell, but they were all full.

What had been a relatively simple questioning at the border turned into a more sinister one at Ferizaj.

The first morning, Sali was taken to a plush office in the police station with three leather chairs, a black shiny table and a tatty, rickety, wooden chair. He was told to sit on the old chair while three police officials settled down into the leather chairs. Straightaway Sali had two shocks.

Firstly, one of the police officers was a Kosovan Albanian whom he knew a little, as he had been at college with his brother. Even worse Sali's father, when he was a town official, had paid the electricity bill of this Kosovan Albanian's father when he was in desperate need.

Secondly, they knew everything about his life – from his schooldays to his Christian conversion in Vienna; from his studies in England to his work in Munich, and, of course, his radio work as Luan Mateu. They were even aware about his invitation to Switzerland for a few days one Christmas to preach to a group of Yugoslavs, of whom 38 of the 41 were Kosovan Albanians.

Suddenly, it dawned on Sali that the incident in Munich when the two men had nearly dragged him into a toilet cubicle was not an isolated one; it was part of a continuing surveillance on him.

What he didn't realise until later was that Albanian officials had written to the authorities in Kosovo to say they had been watching Sali Rahmani for a long time.

However, Sali didn't know anything about that as the questions began.

"What is this radio programme, the Way of Peace? What peace are you bringing?"

They went through every aspect of his life for the whole day, every day. He was not given any food and had only one drink until he returned to his parents' house in the evening.

At this time, there were tensions between the Kosovo Albanians and the Serbs and the Yugoslav authorities and it was beginning to boil over with protests and even bomb attacks.

"Rahmani," the three interrogators went on, "this religious work is just a cover for your political objectives. You are trying to foment unrest in different parts of Europe against the Yugoslav government."

A few months earlier, there had been an attack in Stuttgart when a couple of bombs went off and Sali was accused of being behind that.

"You are working for intelligence agencies in Western Europe and America, aren't you? We know you are a CIA spy."

The questions went on day after day and Sali kept answering that he was a missionary doing God's work and denied any political motives and any links to the CIA.

Even his mother and father were questioned, but the police couldn't find any evidence to implicate Sali.

However, as a couple of weeks passed by Sali began to get worried because no one knew what had happened to him.

His wife, Helen, and his children would be concerned because they would soon be preparing to go to an ECM conference in Germany, and they had had no news from him.

After a couple of weeks, Peter decided to take a chance, to leave Sali's parents' house, and go to the post office to ring his wife. It was risky because there was a queue for phones and everyone could hear what was being said which was presumably passed on to the police. Still Peter managed to get through and asked his wife also to give a message to Sali's wife Helen and ECM's Eastern European director, Tom Lewis. Peter also contacted Sali's friend, Simo Ralevic from Peja, who managed to come over and meet him.

Each day Sali prayed that he would be able to tell his story of why he had become a Christian, but he was never allowed to.

"You are trying to convert us," they sneered whenever Sali mentioned his faith.

"It's not me, but God who will convert you," he replied.

Then the interrogators changed tactics and tried the nice approach. One day only the Kosovo Albanian turned up and he was much softer.

"I am proud of you," he began. "Your family were very kind to our family. I want you to come and work in Kosovo, I can get you a job. First, you have to admit to me that you were involved in these bomb attacks. At the moment your life is in a mess."

Sali replied: "As a Christian, I can't tell you a lie just to please you."

With that the interrogator got up from his chair and hit Sali so hard across his face that he fell back in his ramshackle chair leaving him sprawled across the floor, the chair in pieces and the hot coffee he was drinking all over his face.

When the two Serbian interrogators arrived in the room, they were told that Sali had grabbed the chair and begun to attack the Kosovo Albanian, who naturally had to defend himself.

In turn, they hit Sali and warned him that they were preparing to send him to the High Court in Belgrade, where he would face at least 22 years in jail.

The next session became even nastier as they said they had received information that Sali's wife, Helen, had left him and that she and their children had gone to live with her father in Scotland. Sali, however, knew that they were due to go to the ECM conference in Germany.

They continually accused Sali of propagating the Christian message, mostly through his radio work. But one day they produced a couple of plastic bags with an Albanian John's Gospel in it, plus a large straw to keep the bag afloat, some chewing gum and Christian literature on which there were Sali's contact details.

What do you know about these, demanded his interrogators?

Sali knew about them, but very wisely, he had asked the Christians involved not to tell him too many details. Now he was glad he had been careful.

Some Christians had approached him with an imaginative scheme to get the Christian message into Albania. This group had filled 1,000 plastic bags and dropped them into the 335-kilometre-long River Drin in Kosovo to float downstream into Albania.

Another idea Sali knew of was very foolhardy. Two Americans wanted to buy a huge stack of Sali's Albanian Christian literature, rent two planes, fly over Albania and drop the literature in by parachute. Fortunately, he talked the American pilots out of their outrageous plan, mainly on military grounds. He said that, although the Albanian military was not the best in Europe, they still had enough equipment and training to shoot down two small planes in their airspace.

His interrogators refused to accept that Sali had not had anything to do with this unusual plastic bags mission. They added that it had been a useless enterprise as the authorities had fished all the plastic bags out of the river. So Sali was delighted when he was visiting Christians in Kruje, Albania, about ten years later and one of them produced the plastic bag and Christian literature, which he had found in the river and read.

Meanwhile, Sali was wondering how he could convince them of his innocence, when one of the interrogators let slip the plastic bags had been put into the river on Saturday, June 26, 1976.

Suddenly Sali shouted with delight. "I can prove it wasn't me. I had nothing to do with those plastic bags being dropped into the river. I wasn't even in Kosovo on that day.

"I was a couple of thousand miles away," he said triumphantly. "I was in Glasgow as it was my wedding day."

Peter's courage in making the phone calls had also paid dividends. Tom Lewis, who was ECM's Eastern European director and a friend of Dr Ian Paisley, spoke to the Northern Ireland politician who helped mobilise MPs and Foreign Office officials. Meanwhile, church leaders contacted the Baptist Union in Zagreb, who in turn wrote to the Yugoslav Government.

At the ECM conference in Stuttgart, they were praying for Sali every day and Tom decided to drive to Ferizaj to give Sali and Peter moral support plus the marriage certificate to show the police.

By the fourth week the interrogators relented and let Sali tell the story of his conversion. "You have just ten minutes," they told him. Sali spoke for one hour and 15 minutes.

His interrogators were visibly moved. The Kosovo Albanian told him: "I would wish our young people would be like you. If you need any help, please contact me." With that, he gave him a card with his direct office phone number.

Within two days the interrogator returned to tell Sali: "I have very good news. I have your passport you are free to leave."

When Sali returned home, there was only time for a quick farewell to his parents before they raced off to the border. Tom knew of stories where Christians had been released by the authorities and when they arrived at the border, customs officials had opened their cases and found drugs planted on them.

But Tom wasn't worried about the journey. "I had done far more difficult trips into Eastern Europe previously smuggling Bibles into Russia, Romania, Bulgaria and Czechoslovakia," he said.

Tom drove Sali straight to Vienna so Peter could be reunited with his wife Susi, before taking them all to the ECM conference in Germany.

One of those at the conference who had been praying for Sali's safety was Barbara Jamieson, who had first invited him to go to church in Vienna in 1972.

"It was like chapter 12 in the Book of Acts," said Sali. "Peter was arrested by King Herod, put in prison and then miraculously delivered. He walked straight from prison into a prayer meeting.

"The same happened to me. I went straight from house arrest into meeting people who had been praying for me. It was very emotional."

Nevertheless, although Sali hadn't been able to try to track down any listeners on that visit it didn't put him off trying twice again in the next three years – and each time he was arrested.

Two years later, he returned to his family home in Ferizaj. This time, the same Kosovo Albanian police officer who had questioned him last time interrogated him again.

After four days, he was released and he bumped into his interrogator in the town. To show there were no hard feelings, Sali gave him the kilo of coffee he had brought with him from Vienna.

"He was very grateful and moved by the gesture," said Sali.

This time he managed to travel and meet some of his listeners. His father, Hasan, insisted on accompanying his son, whether it was for security reasons or because he was inquisitive, or both, Sali never found out.

Once they went to a village near Prishtina and met a listener who had written letters to Sali and the radio station.

"My father was amazed by the reaction when a complete stranger greeted Sali as a friend and invited him to a meal in his house. The householder told Sali in front of everyone: 'You are very welcome, you are part of our family, you are here with us every night'."

Later Hasan told his son: "Thank you, I enjoyed the visit very much."

After that Hasan, a former hardline Communist, changed. He never told Sali whether he had become a Christian, but he said to his friends in his street: "God is my friend and I am his friend."

A year later in 1986 Sali had to return home because his father had died. Again, he was questioned for two days, but this time it didn't matter. Because of the distance Sali had had to travel, he had arrived too late for the funeral anyway.

12

THE TIMES THEY
ARE A-CHANGIN'

1989 was the year when both Albania and Berti began to change. The leader of the Party of Labour, the Communist Party, Ramiz Alia, had tried to introduce a programme of cautious liberalisation. However, the people were impatient for change as they had watched the Berlin Wall being torn down that year and seen the old governments of Eastern Europe overthrown. When the Ceausescu regime in nearby Romania fell in December 1989, Ramiz Alia knew he had to speed up the reforms, even though the Foreign Minister defiantly declared: "What is happening in Eastern Europe has nothing to do with us."

Opposition newspapers were allowed for the first time, while new political parties began to form and the ban on contact with foreigners was removed. The following year the death penalty was abolished for most anti-state offences.[13]

However, these cautious movements of change did not satisfy the people who were impatient for more radical ones.

The authorities became nervous as rioting broke out all over the country and they ordered the military to draw up a Rapid Defence Force to quell the riots and to protect public buildings such as town halls, schools, political offices and hospitals from the mobs.

One of those the Defence Ministry called up first was Berti, who was sent to a special base at Kavaja at the end of 1989, ironically the scene of his greatest military achievement where he had been presented with his top medal.

While the units were in training, the political situation deteriorated further. In January 1990, thousands of Albanians fled to Greece and crowds, mainly young people, seized many of the foreign embassies. Then there was the first students' protest on December 8, 1990, which started in Kavaja.

Tanks were stationed on the Albanian streets and Berti's job, as communications chief at Kavaja, was to be the link between the soldiers in the tanks and his Commandant.

Berti admitted the soldiers were unhappy to be deployed against their own people, but they were told not

---

13 *Albania, who cares?* by Bill Hamilton, published by Autumn House.

to confront the protesters who wanted democracy, and to avoid trouble if possible.

He said the situation became more tense when the Albanian Government sent up soldiers from Skrapar, an area three hours to the south, which was still pro Hoxha, to Kavaja, which was anti Communist.

The protests on the streets continued throughout 1990 and into 1991, when on February 21, crowds pulled down the large statue of Enver Hoxha in the central square of Tirana. It was a symbolic image, which was to be repeated 12 years later when crowds toppled the statue of the Iraqi dictator, Saddam Hussein, in Fardus Square, Baghdad, on April 9, 2003.

"That was the day Communism in Albania ended," said Berti.

The political situation was defused in the short term in March 1991 when the first democratic elections in Albania were held, which the partially reformed Party of Labour won, mainly because many of the rural people didn't want change and couldn't see on television what was happening in the rest of Europe.

The new government lasted only two months when a three-week general strike in May forced its resignation and led to a national unity coalition government, including non-Communists.

With food riots and troubles everywhere, the new government put the country on the highest military alert. Reservists were called up and the Rapid Defence Forces were redeployed on the streets again, at the same time as the European Economic Community launched a major aid programme, Operation Pelican, overseen by the Italian Army.

Politicians went on television to appeal for calm, accusing the students of being immature and asking the people whether they were prepared for an enemy invasion, which could happen now, as the borders were open.

As Bill Hamilton, the BBC journalist, wrote in his book, *Albania, Who Cares*: 'By then the country was also in economic chaos, its people queuing sometimes for hours just to get bread. [2]

'To watch the excitement of children walking home with a loaf under each arm, you would have thought they were carrying bars of gold. At night, many of them were sent on to the streets by their parents to set rubbish alight to keep them warm. Firewood was fast running out.

'Along some country roads there was hardly a tree left standing, such was the desperation. The shops were empty – no meat, no fish, no coffee. At one stage, the entire railway network had to be closed down. The general manager feared a disaster. Railway sleepers were removed for fuel, and signalling wire was torn down by those who had thought of an innovative way of connecting electrical supplies from streetlights into their homes.

'Nearly 70 per cent of the adult population were out of work. There were no raw materials for the factories. Machines stood idle and resilience was wearing thin. One electrical worker trying to mend a severed cable was machine-gunned to death by an angry mob. Lethargy had set in with Albanians losing the desire to work and becoming almost totally dependent on Western aid.'

Eventually a third election was held in March 1992 and the Democrats swept to power with more than 60 per cent of the vote. To show how desperate the situation was, a power failure in Tirana on election night meant the ballot papers were sorted by candlelight.

The next day more than 100,000 people filled Skenderbeu Square to celebrate the Democrats' victory and cars drove triumphantly around the city centre until they ran out of fuel.

It was the beginning of a new era as Albania came in from the cold after nearly 50 years of Stalinist isolation. The new president, a 48-year-old cardiologist, Sali Berisha, symbolised this by refusing to move into the Presidential Palace, deciding to stay instead with his family in their two-bedroomed flat on a rundown Tirana housing estate.

It was also the beginning of a new era for Berti. What he had seen on the streets of Kavaja had made him question his military role and his career.

He watched as soldiers used guns to fire over the crowds of people to frighten them. He had been convinced that no soldiers would ever fire, or be ordered to fire, on their own people.

However, their rules said that they had to protect the government at whatever cost, and if necessary, with their lives.

"I had loved my profession, but for the first time I began to rebel at the army's orders. I hadn't joined to do this," he admitted.

He even challenged his superior officers about what was going on. Now Albanians knew there was no enemy about to attack them, they said there was no need to have so many military bases. In addition, the economic situation in Albania meant the military budget had to take its share of cutbacks.

"When I went to the base there were 20 officers hanging around with nothing to do," said Berti. "I said to my commanding officers, 'What are we doing? We will become a lazy army.'"

The problem was that most of them thought it was impossible for them to find work if they left the army, whereas Berti knew he could.

Previously, he had tuned in when he could to the Trans World Radio broadcasts and Luan Mateu's programme. However, with his move to the Rapid Defence Forces he began to listen more often, sometimes recording the programmes to hear them again later.

With the army becoming more disorganised, discipline breaking down everywhere, the government more relaxed and Albanian liberation seemingly not far away, Berti plucked up courage in 1991 to write to Trans World Radio.

By 1991, Berti knew his army career was coming to an end, so he began planning for the future. At the same time, he met up again with his second cousin, Tomorr Dosti, who used to come from Tirana to spend his summer holidays in Lushnje with Berti. Now Tomorr, who was a customs officer at Rinas, Tirana's main airport, also ran a business and he offered to lend Berti some money to open a kiosk.

Since Albania had begun to opens its borders in 1990, there was more money coming into the country, mainly from Albanians working abroad who wanted to help their relatives back home. In addition, Albanians, after years of austerity, were making up for lost time and were hungry for education and goods, such as chocolates, sweets, chewing gum, cigarettes and stationery.

The more Berti thought about the idea of opening a kiosk the more he liked it. He knew he couldn't go back to his previous career of repairing radios. He had spent so much time working on army radios that he was out of date with his knowledge of ordinary radios.

However, a kiosk was an excellent business idea and he knew the ideal location. Nevertheless, he was still in the army and needed a partner to help him run it, and Berti thought immediately of someone who could help him.

He went back to his old friend Ladi, and his 'adopted parents', Leksi and Liri.

Ladi was delighted to join him, while his parents allowed them to put up a kiosk in the corner of their garden on the corner of a busy junction.

It went so well, with Ladi running it in the mornings and Berti looking after it when he had finished his army duties, that they soon expanded by selling groceries and staying open until 10pm to provide coffee. Within 18 months, Berti had repaid the loan to his cousin and there was enough money in the business for Ladi and Berti to buy a car.

13

I THINK I RECOGNISE YOUR VOICE SAID THE GOVERNMENT OFFICIAL

Every radio presenter is always interested to know how many people are listening to his or her programme. However, to Sali Rahmani it was even more basic: Is anyone in Albania listening? It was a question, which ECM had been trying to answer for years. The first people to try were Barbara Jamieson, who worked for ECM in Vienna, and Margaret Willan, who worked for ECM in Munich with the Eastern Europeans.

When in 1975 a Czech charter company advertised probably the first ever holiday to Albania, Barbara and Margaret couldn't resist going. However, even they were a little surprised when they met up with the rest of the group and found most of 30-strong party were German Communists going to Albania to help build a railroad.

Their flight was uneventful until they tried to land at the airport in Tirana, Albania's equivalent to Heathrow in England, and found there were cows on the only runway. In addition, even though it was an airport, there were no other planes.

"The only planes to use the airport were from Communist China, and they landed and took off only on Saturdays and Sundays," recalled Margaret.[14]

Border guards checked their cases and asked them three questions. "Have you any books against our government? Have you any bombs? Have you brought any foreign newspapers or periodicals in the country?"

Their guide was an East German, who told them they couldn't leave their hotel without his permission. He had been brought there so he could translate for the German tourists.

The two women enjoyed their ten-day holiday and had a good tour of the whole country.

However, what stood out for them was the lack of traffic, particularly cars. "Members of the diplomatic corps had cars, but most people travelled by bus, lorry, ox-cart, donkey or bicycle," said Margaret.

---

14 *Albania's Empty-Handed Freedom*, published by the European Christian Mission.

In the small towns and villages, they noted that some people had small transistor radios. "We saw a group of men had placed one in a red cover under a black umbrella and were sitting round it, listening," said Margaret.

However, radios were expensive. One model they saw in a shop, with three wave bands, was priced at 800 lek, which was more than a month's wages for many listeners.

Although they didn't find any listeners to Trans World Radio, they did discover the programmes were going out at the wrong time, when workers were changing shifts. When they returned home, they reported this to Sali Rahmani and the radio team changed the time to beam the programmes into Albania.

Sali knew that the change of time had made a difference in other places. When he went back home to Kosovo in the 1980s, he had proof of that; one of them was now working for him. Since 1987, Rifat Buzuku, a professional boxer, tuned in to Sali's programme from Kosovo and when he moved to Dortmund, Germany, he continued listening.

He came to England to meet Sali, became a Christian and was then invited to work for ECM in Vienna. Rifat sent literature to listeners, replied to their letters, translated tapes and sometimes even wrote his own scripts for Sali's programme, as well as going to Bible school in Austria.

Were there listeners in Albania itself? When ECM held its 1991 conference in Corfu, the Greek island that is only a few kilometres from Albania, the temptation to go there on a day trip was too much for Sali.

There was a two-hour ferry crossing leaving Corfu town port in the morning and returning from Sarande in Albania in the afternoon. As no visas were needed, he persuaded ECM director David Clark and 28 other conference delegates to join him.

The main reason tourists go to Sarande is to visit Butrint. This UNESCO World Heritage site, with an amphitheatre seating 5,000, was mentioned in Virgil's Aeneid and the Letters of Cicero.[15]

That autumn in 1991 Sarande probably had its most unusual tourist invasion as 30 Western Christians arrived singing and giving out literature and copies of John's Gospel in Albanian.

They were inundated with crowds of people, including soldiers wanting to see who they were, to take the gifts and to try out their English.

After the attractive port and seaside town of Sarande, the group moved on to Gjirokaster, Enver Hoxha's birthplace and a UNESCO World Heritage city, famous for its Ottoman buildings, particularly its 13th century citadel.

While the ECM members were walking up to the citadel, they met some teenage girls, who followed them and wanted to practise their English.

---

15 *Blue Guide: Albania & Kosovo* by James Pettifer.

"Have you heard of God and Jesus Christ?" asked David.

"We have heard of God, but who is Jesus Christ?" they replied.

"It was both an exciting and foreboding time, as we saw the beautiful mountains but also the poverty and lots of military bunkers," added David, who was used to forbidden countries.

His parents had been missionaries in China and his father and mother, who was pregnant with him, had to flee from Chongqing in Sichuan Province in Western China when there was a clampdown on missionaries.

After a career as an engineer, he joined the European Christian Mission as a voluntary area representative in 1975 before becoming leader of ECM International in 1993.

Despite Sali's best efforts, they didn't find one listener that day. It would be another five months before Sali found some listeners in a most unexpected place and under unusual circumstances.

In autumn 1991, Dr Janet Goodall had just retired after a successful career as consultant paediatrician in North Staffordshire when she had a phone call from Ron Newby, a social worker, who had set up Global Care, a British registered, international Christian charity helping in Uganda and Romania, when he retired.

When he later saw TV pictures of ships overladen with Albanians fleeing to Italy and naked, emaciated children who were being held in desperate conditions in barren institutions, he knew that had to be the third country the charity would help.

Ron realised he needed a paediatrician to take with him to Albania, so he rang Dr Goodall.

"It was September 1991," recalled Janet, "and Ron was ready to travel the next week. That we had no visas, no local currency nor knowledge of the language did not deter him. He was still prepared to go, even when he didn't receive any answers to his faxes explaining our intentions to some of the government ministries."

Although Janet had agreed to accompany Ron, she was slightly concerned by the lack of planning. However, she was relieved when just a few days before they were due to fly on Thursday, September 26, Ron told her that he had stumbled across an Albanian-speaking Christian, Sali Rahmani, who had agreed to accompany them. Midway through the flight Janet's heart sank when she learned that her interpreter was on the Albanian Government's blacklist because of his Christian activities.

"We set off without visas and not knowing whether we would all three be clapped into jail on arrival," said Janet.

However, there was no chance of Sali slipping unnoticed into the country. As he left the plane and walked over to the terminal, he was so emotional at being in Albania that, in Papal fashion, he fell on his knees, kissed the tarmac, and shouted "Hallelujah" in front of bemused passengers and airline staff.

Although Sali admitted he was very happy to be in Albania, he was nervous about what sort of reception he would get.

There were two surprises awaiting them in the arrivals' hall. Firstly, the officials allowed them into the country with the minimum of fuss and secondly, there were a group of Albanian Christians to greet them and take the visitors by taxi into Tirana.

The Christians had arranged for the three to stay with a young man, Petro, who had agreed to open his flat to them.

Janet, who had the settee in the dining room, said she was amazed to see the walls lined with bookshelves full of volumes of Shakespeare translated into Albanian.

She learnt later that Petro's father was at one time a language professor at Tirana University while his evangelical grandfather had helped to bring back the Albanian language and the gospel to the country. Petro said his grandfather had been invited to dinner by members of the Greek Orthodox Church 'to explain his beliefs' and had died mysteriously shortly afterwards. Petro was convinced he was poisoned, but whether it was that or food poisoning was never proved.

The next day, Janet, Sali and Ron set off to try to meet a deputy minister of Foreign Affairs with whom Ron had been corresponding.

They were invited into the office of Dr Maksim Bozo, who fished Ron's fax out of his shirt pocket and said that he had been expecting them, even though he had never replied to them.

Dr Bozo, whom Janet was delighted to learn was a paediatrician like herself, took them into a beautiful room with a sumptuous carpet. Over coffee, he introduced them to the Minister of Foreign Affairs. The room was full of about a dozen people, the equivalent of Britain's senior civil servants, as Sali began translating for Ron and Janet and explaining why they had come.

Sali was slightly unnerved by a very senior person sitting opposite to him, who kept looking at him and smiling while he was talking.

When there was a break in the meeting the civil servant sidled up to Sali and asked him: "What is your job?"

"I am a missionary, I preach the gospel," replied Sali.

"Have you spoken on the radio, I think I recognise your voice," he continued, to which Sali admitted he did.

"Is your name Luan Mateu?" he asked again. When Sali replied it was his radio name, the civil servant embraced him.

"I am so glad to see you," he said. The official told how he had been ordered by the Albanian Government to monitor the radio programmes for Enver Hoxha, which he did. He later told his bosses that there was nothing to worry about from the broadcasts, but he continued to listen.

"Something has happened to me, thanks to your radio programme," he said.

When they reassembled after coffee, the minister said in front of everyone: "I gather you have a radio name and a real name, but that doesn't matter. We are glad you have a heart for your country and we welcome you and thank you for your visit, even though I gather you have already been visiting us for a long time, in fact every night."

The visit was such a success that Dr Bozo took Janet, Sali and Ron in his ministry car, plus chauffeur, to visit paediatric institutions around the country.

Janet recalled that they spent the days on visits with Dr Bozo and the evenings following the local custom of gathering in the city squares or parks, where parents and their children, dressed in their best clothes, promenaded or sat chatting in groups. It was all very friendly and the three foreigners quickly became the focal point for the Albanians who wanted to practise their English. More importantly, they wanted to know why Sali had come.

"As he explained about his missionary radio work," said Janet, "it was like New Testament times when the Apostles first took the good news around the Mediterranean.

"Sali was soon engulfed in the crowd, delighted to be able to explain in person what he had only so far been able to share by radio.

"In the end," said Janet, "Ron, who was quite a large person in build, had to fish Sali, who was of quite small build, out of the eager throng as he was worried his evangelist might get trampled on."

On the Saturday evening Sali spoke at a big evangelistic meeting in one of Tirana's main halls, where 11 young people became Christians and they were baptised on Sunday afternoon in the nearby lake.

The Bozos insisted on inviting Janet, Sali and Ron to their home for a meal where they learned life was still tough, even if you were a deputy minister's wife. Dr Bozo's wife, Monda, said she had to get up during the night, while there was a reasonably good water supply, to fill the bath for all their needs next day. There were frequent electricity cuts and food supplies were very limited with many bare shelves in the shops.

Janet said she was amazed when she went shopping and watched Monda looking for the best prices for parsley. The standard wage for all employees was $20 a month, whatever their rank in the Government, so even a deputy minister's wife had to be careful with the household budget.

After a few days, Sali returned home as planned. However, Dr Bozo continued the tour, this time bringing along his 18-year-old daughter, Evis, as interpreter.

She had wanted to learn English at school but had been refused because she was told: "It is the language of spies."

However, that hadn't put her off and she had got up every day at 5am for five years to learn English for two hours before going to school. Her tutors were an old-fashioned textbook belonging to her parents and the BBC World Service. The whole family would have been in big trouble had she been discovered, but she succeeded so well she impressed her visitors with her accent and vocabulary – even though they were the first English people she had met.

Although she was Albanian, even Evis was shocked by the awful places where her father took them.

"It was like going back to the days of Dickens," said Janet, "although the institutionalized children had little hope of asking for more.

"The thin gruel that was their staple diet clearly did not nourish them. Although I became all too familiar with malnutrition when I worked in Uganda, I had never ever seen such emaciated white children en masse in Europe."

The infants lay in rows at the bottom of cots, jammed together in otherwise bare, long white rooms and not a toy in sight.

"We found later in some of the better places," added Janet, "that aid had included toys, but these were locked away in cupboards 'in case the children broke them'."

She said the infants' eyes had an empty, unresponsive stare; the backs of their heads were bald, ceaselessly moving back and forth.

"As we approached the toddlers' ward, we could hear the creak of the cots before we went in. We found their occupants standing up, rocking back and forth, with no other form of available play. The few put into a playpen were listless and apathetic, unless they were strong enough to stand up and hang on to the side.

"Evis handed out Smarties, but the children did not know what to do with this unfamiliar confectionery."

Then the group went to the dystrophic unit, where infants went who were failing to thrive.

"I noticed one of the carers with tears in her eyes as she observed our concern," said Janet.

Most carers were poor themselves. In addition, should mothers wish to visit recently-admitted children they were expected to bribe their way in to supplement the very poor pay of the attendants. Even a breast-feeding mother could not stay for longer than a week, if her baby still failed to gain weight, Janet was told.

Equipment was basic, with tin mugs often used instead of bottles, even for young babies.

If the institutions in Tirana were bad, they were far worse in the historic southern city of Berat, a beautiful historical city that has, what many claim to be, the finest large medieval citadel in the Balkans.

There they were taken to the Befatrof, literally translated, The House of the Foolish, a home for mentally handicapped children under the age of 16.

Many of the children there were roaming about, clad in dirty and inadequate rags.

"My abiding recollections of this place are of broken windows, bad smells, terribly battered iron bedsteads with badly chipped enamel, worn-out bedding, rusted and defunct radiators, and the doctor in charge telling us that half the sick children on his acute ward would die within a year," said Janet.

Some years later, the paediatrician recalled that, after the Duchess of York's visit, most of the children were transferred elsewhere and the place was smartened up.

Because Evis had started university that day, their interpreter was Dr Gazim Boçari, a professor of pharmacology, who told them his university laboratory was so devoid of materials that his days were spent concocting an ointment out of onions.

One girl who caught Janet's attention that day was a child of about seven who seemed to have no facial features at all, apart from grotesque, bloodshot dripping eyes with scarred and retracted eyelids following severe burns. Her skin was dark and scaly and one of her hands was badly deformed with flexed and fixed fingers. She was unnecessarily totally blind, her inability to blink having caused chronic infection of both eyes.

When the little girl's mother had died, her father remarried and her stepmother could not stand the child's facial appearance, so she was put in the nearest institution at the age of three years old. She had been given no formal education and could not even count. Her condition was believed to have originated in a house fire, but even that was doubted with village gossip saying it was arson.

At their final meeting with the minister of internal affairs, Ron offered Global Care's help, medically and educationally, to the Albanian Government. In addition, they would send out two nurses to teach paediatric care.

There was a sad and a happy outcome to that meeting. A few months later when a lorry load of aid arrived at the hospital, it was promptly surrounded by about 1,000 Albanians who saw no reason for the 'foolish' children to be given clothing and toys that their own children had never had. So rather violently, they began to help themselves and stripped the aid lorry bare. The alarmed aid workers took the two nurses back to England with them for their own safety.

However, Janet never forgot the badly disfigured young girl, whom she called Lucy. Ron had taken a photograph of her, which was helpful when enlisting the aid of a kind British plastic surgeon.

A few months later, Janet went down to Heathrow to meet a small party off the plane, Ron escorting two girls along the tarmac, interpreter Evis now pushing a little figure in a wheelchair in a navy-blue anorak and red and white cap, pulled well down to hide her shorn head and some of her burns.

The little girl, from one of the poorest Albanian institutions, was admitted for surgery at a modern private hospital in Birmingham, England. However, Lucy didn't come on her own; she brought Albanian head lice to the top hospital.

Lucy had a number of operations, which helped to improve her looks, and both she and Evis returned home to Albania a few months later.

"They climbed into the back seat of my car – and into my life," said Janet, who has continued to support Lucy and kept in touch with her through Evis and her mother Monda. Lucy made such good progress that she was able later to study at a university in Tirana.

14

A LETTER FROM ALBANIA – AT LAST

The government official who met Sali wasn't the only person who had been listening to Luan Mateu's programmes. Early in 1991, the first listener's letter from Albania arrived, 23 years after ECM had first started broadcasting into the country, and 18 years since Sali had begun his programmes.

"I was so excited," said Sali. "I didn't open it for an hour as I was so busy phoning my friends to tell them."

It was from Veria, an Albanian widower in Fier. He told Sali he had been secretly listening to his programme for a long time in the cellar of his home with his 10-year-old daughter.

Veria, who was from an Orthodox background, had made a small altar out of a table and on top had placed the radio and some bread and wine so the two of them could share communion as instructed by the programme.

He wrote: "I was scared my daughter might tell her friends about the programme, but the government officials never found out. I wasn't scared of going to jail, but I was afraid of losing my close friend the radio."

Sali wrote back and invited him to a Christian camp that he, Stephen Bell, and others had been running since 1988 for Kosovan Albanians in Leptokaria, Greece.

In July 1991, Sali was giving a talk at camp when his wife Helen told him an Albanian, Veria, had arrived looking for Luan Mateu.

Sali was speechless. He apologised to the 20 campers and said he had to have a break as this was "a very important day." He rushed over to Veria and they embraced each other. Veria said he had travelled the 300 kilometres in a lorry crossing the Albanian border into Greece, made his way to Leptokaria and kept asking the locals until he found someone who could tell him where the camp was.

Veria spent the week there, returning the same way to Fier as he had come. He later became one of the founding members of the church in Fier.

After Veria's letter, many started to arrive from Albania on a regular basis, including some from Berti. However, even Sali was surprised when in early 1992 he received a neatly written letter from a nine-year-old girl from Lushnje.

Esmeralda Shahini was playing outside her house in Lushnje when she noticed a leaflet on the pavement, which said: "If you are interested in God and Jesus' good news and would like a Bible, write to us." There then followed a box number and the frequency for Trans World Radio's Way of Peace programme. Esmeralda was intrigued, so she wrote a letter and then surprised her mum by asking her for the money for a stamp. Her mother was even more amazed when she told her why. Nevertheless, because she had been brought up in the Orthodox Church and wanted her daughter to continue in the faith, she paid for the stamp. Although it had been illegal to listen to a foreign radio station, and particularly one talking about religion, Esmeralda persuaded her 15-year-old sister Senola and their parents, Llambi and Parashqevi, to join her in listening to the Trans World Radio programme. They enjoyed it so much that they continued listening and soon Esmeralda's Bible arrived from ECM via Trans World Radio.

Eagerly she opened it and began reading. "I read the Bible all the time and really enjoyed it."

Her parents hadn't gone to church for 35 years as Enver Hoxha had forbidden it.

The Albanian leader had been so impressed with China's Chairman Mao and his cultural revolution, launched in August 1966, that he decided to copy him.

Intellectuals were sent into the countryside to work in the factories and farms with the ordinary people. Women were encouraged to join the labour force and religion was blamed for oppressing and exploiting the people in the past.

In 1967, Hoxha said: "Islam has been the ideology of the Turkish occupier. The Orthodox religion has been the ideology of the Greek chauvinists who have occupied the country in the past, and Catholicism – with the Vatican at its centre – has been the ideology of the Italian invaders, Austrian imperialism and Italian fascism."

Years later Berti remembered himself as a 10-year-old watching a mob of about 200 or 300 people demolishing the big Catholic Church in Laç in 1967. Berti Dosti said the local Party secretary led the group of mostly young people to the church armed with sledgehammers. As the mob got to work, the secretary whipped up the emotion, urging them to be more patriotic and more zealous than the crowds in other towns.

Berti said some of them later admitted they were scared, but felt they had to join the crowd. Some suspected there was money behind the icons, while others said believers had seen these holy relics shedding tears. Many refused to touch the icons, thinking it would bring them bad luck.

However, Berti thought many icons had been moved to safety a few nights previously.

Although Enver Hoxha could close religious buildings, he couldn't stop people believing and keeping to their traditions. There were many stories of brave priests who hid their vestments, but continued to carry out their priestly duties and baptised babies.

Worshippers also continued to observe Christmas and Easter in secret, as Hoxha had outlawed these festivals. He wanted the people to concentrate on New Year when a factory or farm would announce last year's achievements and their aims for the coming year.

At New Year, everyone was encouraged to have a family meal at home and the government would help the people by doubling their meat ration just for that week. At the meal, people were expected to drink three toasts with raki, beer or wine. The first toast was that Enver Hoxha and the party would have a long life, the second was to thank everyone that you had had a good life in freedom and with food, and the third one was to wish everyone a happy New Year.

However, many people, like letter writer Esmeralda's parents, Llambi and Parashqevi, chose to celebrate Christmas still in the traditional way, even if they couldn't go to church.

Like many Orthodox families, they would eat hard-boiled eggs at Easter in secret, and paint the shells red to remind them of Christ's blood and death on the cross, and would enjoy a family meal at Christmas and at Easter.

Llambi, who was a chemist in a food factory and Parashqevi, an economist who worked in a plastic factory, said to hide the evidence they would flush the shells down the toilet, while they knew of other families who would bury them in the garden.

Even then, Parashqevi said people had to be careful on feast days. Sometimes Communist officials would arrive unexpectedly on Christmas Day or Easter Day, saying they were checking whether the house was tidy or the bathroom was clean. In reality, it was to see what they were eating, who was there and whether they had bought in special food for a celebratory feast.

Even more deviously, colleagues from work would be sent to call unexpectedly and report on what they had seen.

Esmeralda and her sister Senola continued to listen regularly with their family to the Trans World Radio programme. By 1992, the political situation had eased and it wasn't so dangerous to be seen having an interest in religion. Quite often Esmeralda would invite some of her friends to come round to her house and listen as well.

"I was a little scared," recalled Esmeralda, "but I wanted to know more and more about the Bible." She wrote another three times to the radio station and kept all her replies, plus the Bible and literature they sent.

The family were delighted one day to receive a telegram from Luan Mateu inviting them to come along that summer to Vlorë for the first ever summer camp they were holding in Albania for listeners of the radio programme.

The whole family went along and Esmeralda said: "It was a very special camp. I enjoyed hearing the Bible stories and playing on the beach."

At the end of the week, Esmeralda told Sali: "This is like heaven. Can we do the same things when we go home? I have already asked my parents and they have said yes."

Another early letter writer to ECM via Trans World Radio was Berti. As well as providing a good business, one of the other advantages of the kiosk was that it was a safe postal address for his correspondence to ECM through Trans World Radio.

"What are you interested in?" they wrote back after one of his letters in 1990. "I want to know more about God," said Berti. "The answers are in the Bible," they said. "What is the Bible?" replied Berti, who then asked for one to be sent to him, which they did.

Trans World Radio and ECM also recommended a correspondence course to him, which he persuaded another friend, Kashmiri, a Kosovan engineer at a food factory, to translate.

One day Berti was delighted to receive a letter from England, from a Christian who had marked his Soon Bible Correspondence Course work, a reply he still has today.

It was from Dr Leonard Loose, of Brancaster Staithe, King's Lynn. A former missionary in India he then taught at Fakenham Grammar School until he retired. He helped to mark the Soon correspondence course and gave Berti 194 marks out of 200 and 195 out of 200 for his two papers. He wrote:

"Dear Albert, this is the first Bible study paper that has come to me from Albania. I thank the living God and Saviour Jesus Christ that you had this opportunity to send this letter to me. Your handwriting is excellent, your use of the English language is very good and your answers show you have a clear understanding of what you have read from the Bible."

One day Kashmiri warned Berti: "You had better be careful, people are watching you."

"I hope they are," replied a confident Berti, "I hope they find God."

By now, he was desperate to find out everything he could about God and when he saw an advertisement in a local paper for another correspondence course, in Italian, through a Catholic church in Lezha, he applied – even though he couldn't speak the language.

As well as taking a chance by writing to the radio station, Berti took an even bigger risk by confiding in a friend, Kristaq, who was an army officer in the Rapid Defence Force, asking him to translate the Italian replies into Albanian. They took about three or four weeks to arrive and were brought faithfully to the kiosk by a postwoman, Sadate, who later became a Christian and was baptised by Berti in 2003.

"For the next two years I wasn't a believer with all my heart," admitted Berti. "But I wanted to learn, I wanted to do well on the correspondence courses and to get top marks."

Then in 1992, the government announced the first of its six-monthly military reforms and Berti volunteered to leave the army. Despite him being highly experienced and highly qualified, they agreed to let him go. In July 1992, Berti marched out of the safe world of the military with a guaranteed salary, into the more precarious world of being self-employed.

He continued to run the kiosk with Ladi, while listening to Trans World Radio and kept on with the correspondence courses, as well as looking after his wife and bringing up their young family.

In the spring of 1993, Berti was surprised to receive a telegram inviting him to join a number of Albanians at a camp that June in Vlorë, about a couple of hours' drive south of Lushnje.

It was from ECM via Trans World Radio and signed Luan Mateu.

15

GOD HAS BEEN STOLEN FROM US FOR 47 YEARS

Christians were staggered when, in July 1991, the Albanian government, which just over 24 years ago had 'abolished God', invited Christians to come and show them 'how to live properly.'

The Christians asked the government where they could hold a rally, and were given the keys to the Qemal Strafa, the main football stadium in the capital Tirana, where England had played two years earlier. At the opening event, the Albanian Minister of Culture, Arta Dade, told the crowds: "Our country needs spiritual things."

Christians leaders, including Brother Andrew, who founded Open Doors, the international charity supporting the persecuted church, came. Stephen Bell and eight others travelled together by minibus from Prishtina. They were worried what would happen if border officials discovered their Christian songsheets or New Testaments, and even worse, they were in Albanian, a language despised by the Yugoslavs.

However, as they crossed the Yugoslavian/Albanian border at Hani Hoti, north of Shkodra, they couldn't have had two more different receptions.

At the Yugoslavian side of the border, they mumbled vague answers to officials who wondered why they wanted to go to Albania, carefully avoiding any mention of Christianity.

As soon as they drove the 100 metres to the Albanian side, they were welcomed like long lost friends! As the team all spoke fluent Albanian the armed border guards and customs officials insisted they bring out their guitars and sing some Christian songs – all within earshot of the Yugoslav guards on the other side of the border.

Stephen said: "In Kosovo and Yugoslavia we were very cautious, in Albania we were placed on a pedestal as border guards begged us 'Be our missionaries'."

Sali Rahmani had also been invited to Tirana and he decided to drive with his family from ECM in Vienna to Albania and then on to Greece, where he was again leading the summer camp.

On leaving Austria, the first border they came to was Slovenia. What he didn't know was that on the same day, June 27, 1991, the Yugoslav Army had invaded Slovenia, after their parliament had declared their independence from Yugoslavia following a national referendum.

"When we arrived at the border," recalled Sali, "there were soldiers and cars everywhere." Border guards told them they couldn't go any further because of the dangerous military situation.

"But I have got to get to Albania for a conference," replied Sali, who persisted in trying to cross the border, despite his wife, Helen, begging him to stop and turn around.

In the end, the officials decided to let the family through into Slovenia and see the situation for themselves.

Sali was less than ten minutes in Slovenia when he saw the Yugoslav tanks and soldiers coming towards him and decided it was time for a sharp exit. With a rapid U-turn the Rahmani family headed for the safety of Austria, just making it there before the Yugoslav Air Force bombed the border post.

"I was heartbroken," said Sali. "After all those years of broadcasting to Albania and now when they were holding the first big public Christian meeting for 50 years, I couldn't be there."

Incidentally, the Slovenian Territorial Defence Forces and the police kept the Yugoslav Army at bay. On July 7, the Yugoslavs agreed to a ceasefire brokered by the European Union.

Many Albanians were delighted to meet the Christians and called the campaign Zoti e do Shqipërinë, which is translated God loves Albania. They put up six-metre by three-metre banners and notices all round the capital advertising the event, including in the main square, where Enver Hoxha's statue had been until the crowds pulled it down.

Stephen Bell volunteered to help with one of the 13 open-air preaching groups.

"It was amazing, it was like going back to Biblical times," he said. "There were crowds of people. I had four mornings to preach through John's Gospel in which I had one hour to prepare and then two hours to preach – five chapters each day! There were 13 groups, each with a different person preaching from John's Gospel. I had about 50 people in my group, but it was just a sea of faces. I preached until I got a tap on the shoulder to say it was lunch and time to close the meeting."

The visiting Christians were prepared, bringing with them 50,000 New Testaments, 25,000 St John's Gospels and copies of Floyd McClung's book, The Father Heart of God, all of which they distributed.

Stephen said: "We watched thousands clamour for the word of God taking copies of the New Testaments we handed out, and many became Christians during those meetings."

He added: "Once I was asked to take one big box containing a few hundred New Testaments around the stadium from one exit to another one. I had safely negotiated half the stadium perimeter when someone realised I had Bibles. Suddenly a horde of Albanians jumped all over me grabbing desperately into the box!"

Stephen said he had been warned that they should distribute the Bibles strategically during the two-week campaign, otherwise they would all disappear and those needing them most would have to go without.

"So, I bent right over the box to protect the Bibles, while the crowd of 50 grabbed!" said Stephen. "It became dark as the sun was obliterated by the assailing crowd. I started to fear for my own safety until suddenly I began to feel an easing of pressure and was aware of sunlight. Huge Hank, a six foot six inch Dutchman, who was in charge of the team logistics, had come to rescue me."

Stephen Etches, of ECM, translated the New Testament and then the whole of the Bible into modern Albanian, a language different to any other European language. Work on the first Albanian New Testament had begun in 1819 and it was printed in Corfu in 1827 and reprinted in Athens in 1858.[16]

Stephen finished translating the complete Bible in the early 1990s and a leather-bound copy was sent to the President of Albania, Sali Berisha.

"Stephen was a brilliant linguist and it was a privilege to help him with this task," said Sali. "I just wish I had been there to see the joy of the Albanians as they were given the New Testaments in their own language."

---

16 *A Sacred Task* by John Quanrud, published by Authentic Lifestyle.

Although the Christian campaign had been big news in Tirana with 8,000 Albanians at the stadium, the rest of the country had no idea what was happening, as it did not make the news nor national TV. For Berti and others away from the capital it would be another two years before churches were established in their towns.

Once the euphoria and initial enthusiasm of the big Christian rally was over, the problem was how to start a church in Albania, a country the size of Wales with a population of 3.2 million, where in the words of one Albanian: "God has been stolen from us for 47 years."

In October 1991, Christian leaders decided one of the ways to help the church was to form an umbrella organisation, which they called the Albanian Encouragement Project, which had four aims.

Firstly, to enable organisations and churches to co-operate, but also remain autonomous in their individual ministries.

Secondly, to provide a united group to the Albanian Government and international organisations.

Thirdly, to exchange information and communicate with each other to avoid duplication of work.

Fourthly and the main aim was to help and encourage the Albanian Christians to plant churches and help them grow.

The first chairman of the group was Jack Murray, who was also the ECM international director and who spent one week in every three months going out to Tirana for three years.

Meanwhile, Stephen Bell decided he had to move to Albania to help the new church and on October 1, 1991, he left Prishtina University, having successfully completed his course. When he arrived in Sarande by ferry from Corfu, Greece, he was surprised to be greeted by four soldiers, who all recognised him from the rally in Tirana 177 miles away and who were carrying New Testaments given out there.

"As we entered Albania I was suddenly struck by fear," Stephen recalled. "Where on earth would I find food to eat? All around me was abject poverty and dilapidation. However, as I journeyed on the rickety Chinese bus through the countryside and mountains I was really encouraged by a thought from God. 'See these people, Stephen, my people. They are all alive, aren't they? Wherever you see one of my Albanians, there is surely bread for you within four hours' walk. You'll be okay.'"

As he made his way to the capital Tirana, wondering where he should live, a stranger ran up to him shouting: "Stephen, maybe you don't know me, but I became a Christian in your Bible study group in the park in July."

The 19-year-old student, Klodian, invited him to share his room in his family's home and his parents, Ismet and Violeta, adopted Stephen as a 'son'. Later, Ismet escorted Stephen on his church trips.

One day Stephen was asked to drive a borrowed car 70 kilometres to Elbasan, the industrial town where Berti Dosti had worked as a young man, to show the Jesus film at a believer's house. But when he arrived at Anastas's home, the person who was supposed to bring the film from Greece hadn't turned up. Then Stephen became violently sick, and had neglected to guard the car. As night fell it was robbed – of its windscreen!

The next day Stephen had no option but to drive back over the mountains in the freezing December weather in a car, minus its windscreen, thinking he would have to buy a replacement back in Tirana.

He never dreamt he would see the windscreen again, but two days later, Stephen had his most unusual Christmas present. On Christmas Day 1991, Anastas, plus the car owner and a stranger arrived at his house, having driven the 70 kilometres from Elbasan to Tirana to see him. Anastas had tracked down the thief and challenged him about the windscreen, which he said belonged to 'God's messenger' and warned him about the consequences of his wrongdoing.

"Such was the thief's conviction," said Stephen, "that not only did he apologise, but he brought the windscreen to me in person, asked for my forgiveness, and said he wanted to become a Christian. I forgave him, hugged him and shared one of my Christmas presents from my parents in England with him, a Mars bar – an unknown delight in those early days in Albania."

At the end of 1991 and early 1992 hundreds of missionaries flocked into the country to help set up new churches. A surge of people became Christians over the next 12 to 18 months as the church spread out from Tirana into the rest of the country.

At the time, Stephen said: "Albanian believers are youngish, 18-40 years old and really keen to learn. It was exciting to be with them and they are really excited too about what God is doing in their once closed homeland."

But Stephen needed some help with his church work. This was particularly obvious at the end of the first week of the Vlora August camp in the summer of 1992, when Stephen left to go to Germany to become engaged to Tabita.

The romance had started when Stephen had gone with Sali Rahmani to Stuttgart in Germany to visit Albanian refugees there.

One evening they were invited to bring 20 Albanians to a barbecue at the home of Tabita's Christian family, the Sijantas. Three years later, they returned to Stuttgart and this time used the Sijanta's house as a mission base. Later, when they held a third Christian campaign, this time in Freiburg in Bavaria, they invited Tabita to join the team. Tabita had noticed Stephen, but he wasn't aware of anything until he found out that Tabita had checked with friends whether he was married or not.

They started going out, and eventually Stephen proposed to her, on condition that she should first see what life was like in Albania, so she knew what she was letting herself in for.

Tabita, who had been brought up in Germany, was shocked by the poverty in Albania. She wrote home to her family: "Life here is a little different, we must wait two hours for paraffin, water doesn't come all day, electricity occasionally gets cut off and one must search the 'shops' for food."

Despite all this Tabita said yes to marriage and yes to Albania and the couple began preparing for their wedding on Saturday, April 3, 1993, in Germany.

When Stephen returned to Albania, an excited Sali Rahmani met him and told him that, while he was away during the second week of the camps, three Albanians had been converted and baptised. What's more Gëzim, Lida and Xhovi wanted to continue the camp meetings by starting churches in their home towns of Berat and Fier and they asked Stephen to lead them. He agreed, even though the towns were up to 100 miles away from his home in Tirana.

Two girls around 20 years old began to attend the fellowship at Fier. They came by bus from the town of Patos. Because it was dark after the Fier meeting, some of the believers, including Stephen, arranged to drive them the 11 kilometres back home. Alma, the elder of the two, who had been a radio listener to Sali's programmes, regularly invited her friends to come along. In the end, she asked if Stephen could hold meetings at her parents' house in Patos as she had 15 friends who wanted to come.

"Of course, I said yes, while hastily consulting my diary for more of that precious commodity called time," recalled Stephen.

Twenty-six friends came to that first meeting, 25 of whom were women, plus a 12-year-old boy Bledi, and Stephen, who led the church until 1997.

Interestingly, Bledi, who later went to Italy, then returned to Patos where he became an active member of the church there.

Then in December, Stephen and Sali led three evangelistic rallies in Tirana with hundreds of the guests invited by telegram.

In Christmas 1992, Stephen wrote home to say: "These last four months must be among the most fulfilling and yet demanding of my life."

Stephen had set himself a punishing schedule of going every Saturday to Berat, 75 miles away, to take an adult meeting, and then a children's meeting the following morning, before going on another 30 miles for a similar meeting in Fier. On Monday, he led an adults' meeting in Fier, going back on Tuesday to take a Bible study in Berat and returning on the Wednesday to take a Bible study in Tirana.

Thursday and Friday were spent at home. For the first few months, he had to travel by public transport, but was later able to obtain a vehicle, which made the tortuous travelling over poorly maintained roads a little easier.

As these two churches developed into four in the autumn of 1992, there was then the issue of who would take care of them while Stephen was on home leave from April to November 1993 to get married.

He decided the ideal person was his friend Gani in Prishtina. Gani had been on a three-month Bible course and was excellent at encouraging new Albanian Christians to grow in the faith, as well as answering radio listeners' letters, translating documents and helping new missionaries to adjust to Albania.

However, to do that he would have to persuade Gani to give up a good university job and to get his family to leave Kosovo and to come back to what Gani called 'his promised land of Albania'.

In November 1992, he invited Gani and Adile to meet him in Vlora. To Stephen's surprise, Adile was the more receptive to his plans. "I feel we should say yes and we should start in three or four weeks," she told her husband. Gani was shocked, but agreed and they went home to break the news to their three children.

Understandably, they were not too keen on the idea, nor was a horrified Gani's mother who said to Adile: "Tell him not to go, and don't take the children."

But on January 15, 1993, the family, who were now supported by ECM, left Prishtina by truck and by bus for Tirana.

However, 1993 was a difficult year and a tough baptism for the Smolica family.

Gani said: "I was a spiritual sheep and a shepherd at the same time. I had had hardly any training, so I was learning from Stephen and then teaching others."

Adile said: "It was difficult bringing up the children there." After the relatively good lifestyle in Kosovo, she found life in Albania much harder. "I couldn't find any meat to buy and nowhere was very clean," she admitted.

However, just as they were settling down to life in Tirana, Stephen left them on Sunday, March 14, to go home to England and Germany for his wedding. He handed over full responsibility for the Fier, Berat, Tirana and Patos churches to Gani.

In Germany, everyone gets married formally at a registry office and then those who want to can get married in church afterwards.

Stephen and Tabita had the civil ceremony in Stuttgart on March 30, followed by a church service on April 3. The couple enjoyed the church wedding, but Stephen wasn't impressed by the town hall ceremony, which he considered was "pagan".

"Even before the ceremony started," recalled Stephen, "I think the well-meaning German mayor interpreted my body language as being insolent and not interested in the proceedings."

After the civil ceremony, Stephen and Tabita went shopping for the first time as Mr and Mrs Bell. However, when they returned to Tabita's parents at lunchtime that day, her dad said they had to go to the Town Hall and to speak to the mayor urgently.

As Stephen couldn't speak German, Tabita had to translate. The mayor said he had checked out Stephen on his computer and accused him of being a bigamist, warning him that he could go to jail.

It transpired five years ago, the mayor had conducted a ceremony for a soldier called Stephen Bell and he thought Tabita's husband was the same person.

"He took some convincing that I was a different person," added Stephen, who can now laugh at the incident.

Missionary accused of bigamy – Now that's a headline the author of this book never came across in his 44 years as a journalist. It's a story tabloid papers would have paid good money for.

The couple started married life in Fier in November 1993, where Stephen had found a flat. It had one bedroom, a living room/kitchen and a tiny study and a bathroom with hot water and a modern toilet.

Another bonus was that in return for a small salary a neighbour, armed with a rifle, agreed to look after their car 24 hours a day so it wouldn't be stolen.

16

FACE TO FACE WITH AN ANGRY MOB IN LAÇ

The summer camp in Vlorë in June 1993 hadn't got off to a good start. As Berti arrived at the site, which was used as an orphanage during term time, he was met with blank looks as he announced: "I've come to see Luan Mateu."

Then someone remembered it was Sali Rahmani's nom de plume on his Trans World Radio broadcasts.

The camp had been set up to help churches in the rest of Albania, away from the capital Tirana. Sali, Stephen and Gani had gone through all the letters they had received from Albanian listeners and invited those from Fier, Berat and Lushnje to come along to a two-week summer camp to meet each other, and to receive some Christian teaching.

The trouble was that no one knew how many would turn up. Therefore, when the Albanians received a telegram inviting them to a free holiday, with good food at a nice location, they decided to bring their whole family along.

It was total chaos. By the time Berti, who had left his children with his wife Tatjana in Lushnje, arrived all the beds in the dormitory had gone. Berti, used to military discipline and everything done in an organised fashion, was not impressed. It was difficult to find a place to sleep, and when he couldn't find any food to eat, he said to himself: "That's it; things are so bad I'm going home in the morning."

Having found a small space to put down his bed and not having had the best night's sleep, he got up early and walked down the stairs with his bags.

One of the helpers saw him and rushed to find Gani who just caught Berti as he left the site.

"Why are you leaving?" said Gani, who was meeting Berti for the first time.

"I don't like anything here, and besides it doesn't seem like a camp," he replied.

Gani knew if one person left on the second day, others would follow and the whole campaign to reach Christians in the south of the country would fail disastrously at the first attempt.

Thinking on his feet, Gani said: "Stay for my sake, I will arrange things for you."

Gani was as good as his word. He found a bunk bed with the foreign team of camp workers, sorted out the food problem and introduced Berti to Sali.

Berti was impressed and felt so privileged he decided to stay. As he admitted later, it was a turning point in his life.

He soon adjusted to camp life, enjoying the daily routine of breakfast, then worship and Bible study before going to the beach. After lunch, there was time to relax, before another Bible study and an evening service.

Sali said later he couldn't fail to be impressed by Berti, a model student, who took studying so seriously and asked many profound questions, as he had done in his letters to the radio station. He had also brought along the certificates from all his various correspondence courses.

At the Bible study, the first to arrive was always Berti. With his military background he was immaculately dressed, not a hair was out of place and he was eagerly awaiting the lecturer to begin with his Bible and notebook ready.

Berti said that in all those years listening to the radio he had heard about worship, about taking communion and praying to God.

"But suddenly at the camp, things I had heard about on the radio were happening all around me, and I began to understand. I was with other Christians and I started to think differently," he recalled.

By the end of the third day, Berti had forgotten all about the bad start to camp and was now enjoying everything.

However, on the fourth morning he had a rude awakening at 5.30am. His kiosk partner, Ladi, was outside, sounding his horn. When Berti went out to see him, he said: "You've got to come; your brother Iliri has had an accident."

He didn't know any more details, but he went to see Sali and to say for the second time in four days that he was leaving camp. This time Sali knew it was more serious and they said a quick prayer with Berti. Before he dashed off, they asked him if they could visit him at his house, as they knew he wouldn't come back to the camp.

"Yes, you are very welcome," said Berti, before rushing off for the seven-and-a-half-hour journey to Laç, stopping off in Lushnje just long enough to pick up Tatjana, who had been all set to go in the opposite direction to Korçë to visit her family.

Tatjana had had the TV on, but wasn't watching it when the announcement came that a police officer had been injured in Laç. It was only when Iliri said what had happened that Tatjana recognised the voice and turned round to see her brother-in-law on TV. Iliri, who had retired from the army two years ago and had joined the police, was walking in Laç, when he saw two people pushing a woman into a car. Although he was in uniform but not on duty, he tried to stop the car. When he leant in to grab the car keys, one of the men stabbed Iliri twice, once in the ribs and once in the lung. Iliri fainted in the road, while the others drove off.

By the time Iliri was taken in a helicopter to the hospital at Lezha, word had spread around the town claiming that the police had beaten up two people. A crowd gathered, called a general strike and surrounded the police station.

"When we arrived," said Berti, "the roads were full of people with rocks and stones. There must have been a few thousand people on the streets. We were very afraid, but we still didn't know then all that had gone on. People were very aggressive and they were putting up barriers to blockade roads,"

If they had known Berti was Iliri's brother they would have attacked him as well. Some knew Iliri had a brother in Lushnje, but fortunately, no one realised Berti was driving through a hostile crowd in a car with Lushnje number plates.

It was only when Berti and Tatjana arrived at Iliri's house that neighbours told them what had happened.

They urged the Dostis to leave at once, and not let anyone know who they were, or why they had come. They had been told Iliri had been taken to the hospital in Lezha, where his wife's family lived.

Again, Ladi drove from Laç to Lezha, a journey that Berti had done as a young child in a lorry when his father had moved military base.

Frustratingly, when they got to Lezha Hospital, they found Iliri had been taken to Tirana from Laç, which meant a drive of almost another hour.

After a week in hospital, Iliri's lung recovered and he was able to go home. Berti also returned to Lushnje, but by then it was too late to go back to camp. However, the Christian leaders were so impressed in the short time they had seen Berti that they decided to let him run the camp the following year.

As for the crowd in Laç, the police called for the Rapid Response Force who cleared the streets.

However, the bad feeling between the police and the local people lasted for months.

Iliri was reprimanded for interfering when he wasn't on duty. He was demoted to sergeant, not allowed to go back to work in Laç and sent to Lezhna where he became very bitter with the way he had been treated and retired two years later in 1995.

17

A TEARFUL REUNION

Berti had never thought about his mother that much – until he had a strange dream in July 1992. As he had not seen Antoneta since he was three years old, he had very few memories of her. He could hardly remember what she looked like, particularly as he didn't have any pictures of her, and had not seen her, nor even tried to contact her for the last 32 years.

Berti doesn't know why his mother suddenly came into his mind. Whether it was because he was questioning everything in his search for faith, he was not sure. But he knew that it was a vivid dream.

"She was dressed in black," recalled Berti, "she was wailing and I saw her face to face across a room. She said to me 'why don't you meet me, why haven't you tried to find me?'"

When Berti woke up, he tried to convince himself he didn't believe in dreams. Besides, he had been brought up in Communist Albania where anything supernatural or paranormal was laughed at. The authorities said God didn't exist, so obviously He wouldn't speak through dreams. They said no one should believe in superstitions, particularly in the 20th century, and certainly not someone trained as an officer in the Albanian Army.

But the dream wouldn't go away. "What if he did try to find his mother," he said to himself one day. The more he thought about it, the more he realised how difficult it would be. Where would he start?

He didn't dare ask his father because he had forbidden Berti to have any contact with his mother. He didn't know where she lived. In addition, his mother could have remarried and changed her name, or she might not even be alive.

Besides, if he did try to contact his mother he would be going against his father's will, something which was unacceptable in Albanian family life. His father had warned him: "If you meet your mother, you can forget me. I won't talk to you ever again."

Berti knew he couldn't go to any relatives for help as they would immediately tell his father. Moreover, he couldn't go to his older brother, Iliri, who had been told by the family that she was a bad mother, and he had believed them.

Despite all the problems and barriers, he decided he ought to make one attempt to find her. If he didn't, he might regret it for the rest of his life.

Berti booked a fortnight's leave and headed with Tatjana to Korçë, the only place he knew his mother had lived, and so the obvious place to start the search.

It was strange coming back to the place of his birth. He hadn't returned there for more than 30 years, apart from a brief visit to market with his stepmother's father when he thought he might have seen his mother in a crowd.

Despite it being a long time since he had been in Korçë, he did manage to find the neighbourhood where they used to live, with a general store on a street corner. He went in and saw a woman, who must have been about his mother's age behind the counter, so asked her: "Excuse me, do you know Antoneta Dosti?"

The shop woman went pale, was silent for a long time, and then without looking at Berti, said: "No, I don't know that woman."

Berti thought it was very strange, but thanked her and left. What he didn't know until much later was that the shopkeeper was a good friend of Antoneta's, but she had been too frightened to say anything.

He had a vague memory that his mother had worked as a waitress, so he went to the town's biggest bar, the Agimi.

He spoke to one of the staff, who to his amazement said Antoneta had worked there, but didn't now. She thought that she still lived in the house where Berti had lived as a baby and gave him the address.

Fortunately for Berti the neighbourhood hadn't changed that much as the houses were older and had the equivalent to preservation orders on them, so he soon recognised his old home.

But what should he do next? He observed the house for some time and saw a man and then a younger man leave, but he still wasn't sure about going up to the door.

He decided to persuade some children to knock on the door to check his mother was alone.

When she answered Berti recognised his mother, and a few minutes later, he went and knocked on the door himself.

As soon as she answered, she recognised him and invited him in.

She didn't want to show any emotion in public, but as soon as he was inside, she hugged him and cried.

"Why didn't you come before, I have waited so long?" she sobbed. They hugged for some time and then she fainted. Berti didn't know what to do, so placed her on the settee and fortunately, a glass of water soon revived her.

They then told each other what had happened in the intervening years. Berti talked about his upbringing, his time at school and in the army before mentioning his marriage and their two children, daughter Alta and son Dorian.

He said he had lived with his stepmother, who worked as a polisher in a carpentry business, from the age of six to 14, when he went away to school.

Antoneta explained that she had tried to contact him, had sent him clothes and sweets on his birthday for many years, but the parcels had always been returned unopened.

She knew he had moved to Lushnje and had asked people she knew: "Can you find anything out about my Berti?" But they never came back with any news. She spoke to her relatives, but they were scared of Berti's father who said: "Don't tell her anything."

Antoneta said she had remarried, later had a son, and was now a grandmother with two grandchildren. She said when she first met her second husband, he had promised that he would allow her to meet Berti again after they got married. But Antoneta said he became very jealous and possessive, later forbidding her to try and track down her son. She admitted it had not been a happy marriage.

After an emotional hour of swapping news, Berti thought he had better return to Tatjana, who had been waiting patiently for him. As he left, his mother made him promise that he would come back and see her again.

Over the next 12 months, they managed to meet secretly, either at the hotel or in the houses of friends.

However, his father eventually found out and told his other son Iliri. The next time Berti met his father and brother it was a stormy meeting.

"Why have you betrayed me?" demanded his father. "We looked after you because of her."

Berti tried to explain to them both: "I haven't betrayed you, but I just wanted to meet my mother."

As the row continued, Berti told them: "I haven't lost the love for you. But no one can stop me meeting my mother."

However, his father wouldn't accept any explanation and on top of that, the jealousy of his mother's second husband and their son stopped his mother meeting Berti for another three years.

Despite all this, Berti was glad he had found his mother again and has kept in touch with both his parents.

However, he never mentioned the meetings ever again to his father. "I left it with God, there was nothing more I could do," recalled Berti.

18

STARTING A CHURCH FROM SCRATCH

On Friday, July 23, 1993, at 6.30pm the church in Lushnje was resurrected after a gap of nearly half a century.

Following the camp at Vlorë in 1993, the missionaries decided to set up a church in Lushnje and asked Berti and others to gather as many friends as they could.

The first meeting was held in Llambi's house, as their daughter, nine-year-old Esmeralda Shahini had written to Trans World Radio and the family had enjoyed the camp so much. There were 16 people at the service, including Llambi and his family, some of their neighbours, plus Berti and his friend Kashmiri, who had helped translate his correspondence course.

The first service was a very simple one and was led by Sali, Gani and a Dutch missionary Arnaud (whose name means Albanian in Turkish). It included singing and guitar playing, prayers, Bible reading and a talk. During the service, the leaders asked the Albanians to say how they heard about the radio programme, and then suggested they meet again in a week's time when they would also start a children's meeting.

The next service was in Berti's house and, within a month, it was held there every week. Despite all that had happened with the radio broadcasts and the camps, it was no easy task starting a church in Lushnje. Of all the Albanians who came to the first service, only Berti and his children turned up for the second one.

Nevertheless, Gani and Arnaud, who came from Tirana, two hours' drive away every week, persevered. After the service, they slept at Berti's house before returning home the next morning. Even though she wasn't a Christian then, Tatjana said she didn't mind opening their house up and entertaining the visitors.

After the first meeting, they decided to ask Berti, because of his good organisational skills, to set up and lead the service. Berti taught the children while the missionaries took it in turn to preach.

Gradually numbers increased, and as Berti and Tatjana's home became too small, they began to look for a room to rent for the church.

In Lushnje, they found a dental clinic, where 50 people worked in 20 rooms. On the third floor was a large room used for meetings, which Berti's friend, Dr Gjergji, helped them to rent.

On Christmas Day, 1993, at 11am, the new Lushnje church, now called the Way of Peace Church (in Albanian Rruga e Paqes) after the name of the programme on Trans World Radio, celebrated the first service there. A total of 25 people attended, already a healthy increase on the 16 who had met at the first church meeting only five months ago.

The centre was ideal in every way, bar one, which was the entrance. To get there, worshippers had to climb three sets of stairs, which were usually splattered with blood from the patients leaving after having had their dental treatment.

Communist Party officials had used the same room in Enver Hoxha's time. Workers came there to study Hoxha's books, to discuss and underline passages and then to memorise them, finishing by saying praises to Enver Hoxha.

Now Christians were there to study God's word, to discuss and underline passages from the Bible and to memorise verses before finishing by saying and singing praises to God.

For the next few years, Berti continued to listen to the Way of Peace programme on the Trans World Radio station and to study their correspondence course, on top of working, looking after his family and the church.

As well as running his kiosk, in March 1994, Berti also had a job as a waiter in a nearby café. But the owner wouldn't let him have a lunch break to go to a church Bible study. So, the missionaries and local Christians came up with a novel solution. They would have a coffee at the café and talk about the Bible with Berti there.

He left the job in May that year to become an assistant to a lawyer and, although he couldn't type, he had an excellent tutor in Tatjana, who was doing a similar job in the town court. Berti became a court official, but it lasted only three months as he was made redundant because of government cutbacks.

The next day, the wife of the lawyer he had been an assistant to called him. She had been so impressed with his work for her husband that she offered him a job typing legal documents. Although Berti didn't realise it then, it put him in a strategic position to help the victims of the pyramid selling scandal, which would hit the country three years later.

By now, the ECM missionaries had set up six Rruga e Paqes or Way of Peace churches. They were: Tirana (overseen by Gani); Fier and Berat (Stephen Bell); Vlorë (Stephen led this church until Peter and Marie Hoffman moved there in May 1995); Patos (Stephen led this church until Murray Cotter took over in 1997) and Lushnje (Gani led until November 1993 when Berti took over, becoming the first Albanian to oversee a Way of Peace church).

Starting up churches was not easy, but an even more difficult task was to train the Albanian leaders, who had had no Christian teaching.

Sali and Stephen decided the first step was to bring all the church leaders together in Berat on November 17, 1993.

At their first meeting, they talked about training, growing as a Christian and church life and Stephen was so impressed by Berti that he offered to teach him how to preach.

"It was a memorable conference," said Berti, "as I made a public stand about my faith to a large audience."

The following summer Tatjana and the children decided to go for the first time to the Vlorë camp, which Berti was leading. The camps were proving hugely popular, 120 came in 1992, rising to more than 250, the following two years.

It was also a turning point for Tatjana. "I became a Christian there, and it changed my life," she said. "I feel such a different person now."

Every week for a few months Berti travelled to Fier, an hour's car journey away, for a teaching session at Stephen's house. In April 1994, Stephen decided Berti was ready to preach his first sermon. Until then Berti had led the services, but a missionary had always preached. Berti remembers his first sermon on Colossians. First, he wrote it down, sent it to Stephen, and then went to Fier to speak it to him, before preaching it to the Lushnje congregation.

"I was a little nervous preaching at first," said Berti, "but then I became more confident and really enjoyed it."

However, his teacher did not attend the Lushnje service as he and his pupil both agreed it would be too emotional an occasion.

Stephen recalled: "I was very privileged as I watched the Albanian Church grow. I am one of God's workers, yet in a sense a mere bystander 'watching' the Albanian church as it grows. Although it is God who plants churches, we His servants must work our socks off in an attempt to keep pace with His initiatives."

Stephen, Gani, Sali and other missionaries certainly did work hard.

Sali and Gani were travelling down from Tirana every week to Lushnje, while Stephen came from Fier where he had moved to after he had married Tabita, and they all clocked up the miles to help the infant Albanian church.

Meanwhile, Tabita was also busy. In October 1995, she passed her final exam to qualify as psychologist and the following year on August 7, she gave birth to their first daughter, Sheona Naemi. It wasn't an easy time for the proud parents, as baby Sheona suffered from pneumonia for the first two weeks of her life, but then made a full recovery. With a third member of the Bell household, they decided their fourth floor, one-bedroom flat was too small, so in October 1996 they moved into a bigger home in Fier, complete with a garden of lemon and orange trees and vines. The other big advantage was they now had a wall and yard to park their jeep without having to pay armed guards.

Stephen also realised that the Albanian church leaders needed more teaching and three major initiatives were introduced in 1994.

Firstly, ECM decided that pastors and elders from the churches should form a denomination council, which would oversee the churches and approve such matters as the appointment of new deacons, pastors and elders.

Secondly, the board would try to maintain unity among the churches.

Thirdly, it was decided to set up an Albanian Bible Institute (ABI). The country had been open to non-Albanians for about a year and churches were growing fast, at 300% a year, so training the leaders and pastors was a priority.

In a joint venture with three missions – Ancient World Outreach, the Greater European Mission, and ECM – they decided to start the Albanian Bible Institute. The first job was to find a co-ordinator, and they chose Barth Companjen, a Dutchman from Ancient World Outreach, who was an acknowledged Balkans expert.

But who should be the director and dean of studies? The answer came very quickly.

Frans Blok, who was Academic Dean of a Bible School in Holland, said: "We felt God calling us to the mission field and Albania specifically. We did not know much about the country, but decided to send a fax to the office of Barth Companjen in Greece."

This was a guesthouse and office, which served almost all the foreign missionaries in Albania in the first two chaotic years after the country opened up.

"In this fax we mentioned our calling for Albania, our willingness to do what was needed, and our experience with the Bible school," he added.

"Barth came back from Albania after a 14-hour trip by car and the first thing he found in his office was our fax from Holland. You can imagine how surprised and excited he was about this quick answer to his prayer."

Frans was appointed director and dean of studies and he, his wife and three boys arrived in Albania in the summer of 1993.

"For two weeks, I or another itinerant teacher would teach in different cities," he said. "Churches would have everything organised and there would be 20 to 80 students waiting for us. It was also very much appreciated by missionaries as we gave them complementary Bible teaching on top of what they had managed to fit into their busy schedules."

In 1994, ABI moved to a base in Durres, where they rented a school building. It started residential programmes in September 1996 and bought the building in 1997, helped by ECM who gave 50,000 American dollars.

"Our Bible school was geared toward church leaders, with one week in school and two weeks out," continued Frans. "This way they could still lead their churches while being students. Some of them were already pastoring churches, while others assisted missionaries in doing so."

Berti and 15 other key Albanians were the first to be invited to enrol on a three-year course. For one week in every three, Berti lived in Durres, which was an hour and a half's drive away from Lushnje, and attended the lectures. The other two weeks he spent time writing essays, reading the textbooks, as well as fitting in family and work, plus running his church.

Frans particularly remembers Berti Dosti, who was in the first group of students and was older than the others were. "He was great in helping us to understand Albanian culture," he recalled.

It was a big commitment for Berti and the other Albanians. Though no one knew how costly it would be two years later in 1997, when anarchy gripped the country and gunmen controlled the streets of Albania.

1997 – A BAPTISM OF FIRE

If the new Albanian church expected a few quiet years to consolidate, nothing could have been further from the truth. The year 1997 was a very difficult time, with an economic scandal bringing down the government, a civil war, anarchy on the streets as citizens carried guns for protection, and most of the missionaries having to leave the country for their own safety.

If the new church could survive all that, then it could face the future with confidence. As the Albanian Christians look back now, many would say that year was a turning point.

Between 1994 and 1996 there had been rapid economic growth in Albania, with money coming into the country, particularly from Albanians living abroad. People were keen to make up for years of austerity, and were tempted to invest in financial institutions offering unrealistically high rates of returns. To keep these high rates of return, banking 'pyramids' developed, and new investors had to be found so their capital could meet existing liabilities. It is believed that up to two thirds of the population, including many Christians, invested in what was known as Ponzi schemes, with some even selling their home so they could invest more.

The pyramid schemes, offering high interest rates, were a temptation to all. Berti sometimes tried, and failed, to persuade people not to sell their homes as they came to the solicitor's office with their documents to finalise the sale.

"Why are you selling? Are you doing the right thing?" Berti would ask, but by then they were all determined to go ahead with the deal.

Even members of the church joined the schemes. Tatjana confessed she had put a small amount of money in, without telling Berti, when she and the staff at the court decided to invest one day.

Also Berti had opened a small account to help his brother.

In October 1996, the Albanian Government ignored the International Monetary Fund's warnings as investors began to lose confidence, withdraw money and financial institutions started to collapse. In November, the Albanian president, Sali Berisha, went on TV to try to allay people's fears and told them that Albanian money was the cleanest in the world.

That only worried the people even more. They thought somehow that the Government was behind the pyramid scheme.

On January 4 and 5, 1997, Berti said there were long queues as people tried to withdraw their money. The next day the financial scheme leaders disappeared, the system collapsed, and thousands of angry Albanians took to the streets, after losing all their cash. It is estimated that the Albanian people lost the equivalent to 1.2 billion American dollars.

But not quite everyone lost money. Alma and her husband, Drini, invested some money in the pyramid scheme and a few months later decided to buy a house. They withdrew the money – and the profits – just in time.

Eventually, most of the pyramid scheme leaders were arrested by Interpol, tried and then imprisoned. But the vast majority of the Albanian people didn't get their money back.

Things then came to a head politically. One of the first towns where trouble erupted was Lushnje, which was where the pyramid scheme had begun. On Saturday, January 25, crowds began to vent their anger against the Government, which they felt should have protected them. Enraged investors went on the rampage, even attacking the Foreign Minister, Tritan Shehu, when he visited the town. When Berti made his way to church at the top of the dental building the next day for the 11am service there were thousands of people in the town centre. Some were there out of curiosity, but many wanted revenge on the Government, and were systematically setting fire to all the municipal buildings, including the court.

Berti wondered what he could do. He thought he would have to cancel the church service, as he didn't think anyone would dare turn up. However, he thought he would make his way to the top floor of the dentists' building and see if anyone was there.

When Berti arrived at the church he was amazed; the room was full with 30 people. He decided to change the agreed service and lead a prayer meeting instead.

Outside, the people of Lushnje were on their knees economically, while inside, some of the Christians of Lushnja were on their knees spiritually.

At the same time as the prayer meeting, thousands of people were clashing with riot police and setting Government buildings alight in Tirana and other towns and cities across the country.

After an hour, the Lushnje church meeting finished and the Christians carefully made their way home, through even bigger crowds.

As Berti and Tatjana picked their way through the mob, the people didn't realise what a brave service the couple had done already for the town.

Knowing there was going to be trouble, Tatjana and others had been up early, gone to the courts in a car with their boss, entered the offices and taken away the important documents for safekeeping – and all by 7am.

Berti had done the same by collecting the vital documents from his solicitor's office and storing them in a safe place.

During February, thousands of citizens all over the country continued to gather daily to protest and by March, it had become even more violent. Rioters took control of the town of Sarande, seizing weapons, including Kalashnikovs and even tanks, from police headquarters and army barracks, as the local military stood by and watched. Most of the southern half of the country fell into the hands of rebels and criminal gangs, while more than 10,000 people fled to Italy, which in turn, caused a governmental crisis in Rome. Several high Albanian Government officials, including the Defence Minister, Safet Zhulali, fled abroad. On March 2, President Berisha declared a state of emergency as foreign embassies began to send their nationals back home for safety.

"It was anarchy for the first few months," said Berti. "It was very dangerous to go out on the streets, as there were even teenagers with guns and many, many people were killed.

"Schools and factories were closed and people couldn't go to work, even if they had a job to go to."

Many Christians in Berti's church asked him: Should Christians carry guns? Many of them felt unsafe without a weapon, but Berti, who had been trained to use weapons in the army, always advised his church members against it.

However, the problems were brought home to the Christians a few weeks later when a couple of armed gunmen threatened about a dozen of them – while they were having a Bible study.

The first time they took the speakers from the church room and Berti saw no point in trying to stop them. He had to caution a couple of teenagers in the church who wanted to get some guns and go after them. Over the next few weeks, the gunmen came back and stripped the room of everything, including even the radiators.

Berti and the worshippers realised that they had to find a safer building. A believer offered his home, which was on the fourth floor of an apartment block, and they met there until the political situation settled down.

The roads were dangerous too. Gangs were stationed along them, like modern day highwaymen, to hold up and rob people even in their cars – and on the buses.

Despite the dangers, Berti was still determined to continue his Bible course at the Albanian Bible Institute, and he continued to go regularly by car to Durres.

"I was nervous," admitted Berti, "and Tatjana was always glad to see me back home. But God protected me and my car was never attacked, although I did see people who were."

An even bigger challenge was when ECM delivered 24,000 American dollars to Berti, who was the leading pastor for all the Way of Peace churches. This was to buy a house, which was to be the new church in Fier.

But how was Berti to get the money to Fier, an hour's drive away, when he could not guarantee he could get there safely? Even the banks weren't considered a safe place, so he couldn't deposit the money there.

Using his military expertise and planning he hit upon his solution. One night, Berti reversed his van as close as he could to his apartment stairs. To the outsider it looked as though he was repairing the back doors of his van. In reality, he was unscrewing the linings to hide the money inside the door. Next day he drove down to Fier to hand over the money to the owner of the house that the church had bought, and returned with the signed contract. "I was relieved to get back home that day," admitted Berti.

Where the house owner put the money, Berti doesn't know. However, he said many people dug a hole and hid money in their garden.

Although life was dangerous for Albanians, it was even worse for the missionaries who were obvious targets as they stood out from the crowds, and had more money than the locals.

With a heavy heart in March 1997, ECM and other Christian organisations pulled out most of their workers for their own safety. Of the 600 or so missionaries in the country, about 550 left, with all of them worried about how the new, young Albanian church would survive. Fortunately, many were able to return three months later.

Stephen Bell recalled the terrible times as the missionaries escaped by whatever way possible. Stephen said of his family: "We became refugees, fleeing explosive Albania on March 11. Many missionaries left in awful circumstances, but we went out in style on the last car ferry across the Adriatic to Italy, even stopping off for a family pizza at a restaurant on the way to the Durres port!"

Some were taken by helicopter to Rome, some drove to Greece, while Gani and Adile Smolica, plus their four children, flew to Turkey.

Stephen, worried about the church, did fly back the following month. He said in a letter home to his parents: "I was able to be in Albania from April 17 until May 11. I went alone by plane so as not to risk the car being stolen in chaotic Albania. However, it was not as bad as I thought it could be.

"Sure, to an outsider's eye, it was mayhem, but those who had experienced the February and March problems, we are thankful for small mercies. There is shooting at night, but this is mostly friendly fire, usually neighbours shooting into the sky, declaring to potential thieves that they were armed and were no easy prey.

"There are people being killed alas, daily, but these casualties can be put into three categories: a. Mafia robbers fighting with other robbers and Mafia; b. Revenge killings, often Mafia linked; c. Accidents, usually involving children.

"However, there was very little looting and no highway robberies as in March. Of course, in the 'rebel' south (Vlorë, Sarande and Gjirokastar) anything still goes."

But Stephen said he was encouraged how the churches had survived, and in some cases grown.

He said: "During my three-week visit I had two main goals – to show my face as much as possible and go to as many meetings as I could to prepare the churches to be more independent and to be able to face the future, maybe without missionaries.

"In Fier numbers were up and I noticed they were generally enthusiastic, giving friends and neighbours hope in a sad world.

"I spent a couple of Wednesday nights at Berti's house, going to two Bible studies. They had done well; the fellowship was enjoying its most successful spell during its four years in existence.

"New people had come and the challenge was now to teach them. Berti was very encouraged, although he was under a great personal workload and got up at 5am."

Although Berti had heard of a few churches closing, some Albanian believers who had not done any studying, volunteered to help the leaders. By throwing them in the deep end spiritually, the churches had grown, attracting visitors worried about the political situation.

Berti said: "It was a real test for the Albanian leaders and believers, and overall they did well."

At the end of April, Stephen visited two missionaries in Vlorë, who had decided not to leave Albania, Peter Hoffmann and Mark Nyberg.

Peter was helping with the Way of Peace (Rruga e Paqes) fellowship there and Mark was the director of the orphanage. Both recounted harrowing details as to what life had been like during the past two months.

When their year's supply of food had been looted and they had only one week's supply left, they had no choice but to try to get to the Greek border, three hours' drive away.

There they could buy badly-needed supplies for the 65 orphans in their care and could pick up the 27,000 American dollar wages for the 50 workers, who had not been paid for three months.

"As they travelled, they were held up and threatened by armed assailants on numerous occasions, but they got through," said Stephen. "Believers from the church slept at the two town orphanages and also at the missionaries' houses, keeping armed guard."

Stephen had an unusual group to protect his own house. He and Tabita had left in March and soon afterwards, robbers arrived.

Then the 'Triangle' sprang into action. The 'Triangle' consisted of three elderly neighbours – Mihallaqi who lived opposite Stephen, and two 60-year-olds, Zani, next door, and Tarif, on the other side of the Bells – and they arrived on the scene complete with Kalashnikovs and challenged the would-be thieves.

For the next four weeks, they guarded the house, shooting into the sky in time-honoured style, while believers from the church occasionally slept there.

When the Bell family returned to their home, as a sign of appreciation, they invited the 'Triangle' members into their garden for sausage and chips.

"They vowed no thief would threaten me nor Tabita nor Sheona again," recalled Stephen.

There were also other lighter moments for those left behind, as Mark recalls.

Vlorë, where the orphanage was, was firmly under Mafia control with a local 'Godfather' and a few hundred of his armed men.

Previously, Mark had been having problems from a neighbour, who had threatened him with a Kalashnikov, objecting to an extension the orphanage was planning to build. Coincidentally, 15 minutes later, after a difficult meeting with the neighbour, the Mafia Godfather came along, with an entourage of 10 cars, full of 20 men plus Kalashnikovs, bombs and grenades. The Mafia leader offered Mark 1,500 eggs for the children, as he was obviously pleased with the work they were doing, and commented that if he had any problems, he should phone him directly.

As the Godfather departed, Mark told the workers to spread the word that the Mafia leader was so upset neighbours wanted to hinder the building of the new orphanage extension.

Within 10 minutes, a sweating neighbour ran up to Mark, saying that he now had no objection to any building and he would be willing to help with the project in any way possible.

Meanwhile, worried that this anarchy would lead to mass emigration to Western Europe, the United Nations authorised an international military force of 7,000 soldiers under Greek and Italian leadership, codenamed Operation Sunrise, to direct relief and restore order. They arrived on April 15, the same month as a transitional Government was formed. Elections were held in the following June and July, President Berisha was voted out of office and the Socialists took power with Rexhep Mejdani elected president. By August, all UN forces had left Albania and by the autumn the new Government reckoned they controlled most, if not all of the country again.

The only problem was that an estimated 3,000,000 weapons stolen from the army then made their way north into the hands of the underground Kosovo Liberation Army (KLA), which was fighting a major guerrilla campaign against the Yugoslav army units and Serbian police. The repercussions of that move were to have a major impact on Albania in the next 18 months.

20

VICTORY AFTER A YEAR OF ANARCHY

At the end of 1997, the country began to return to normal, but there were huge economic problems with high unemployment and many young people, including Christians, emigrating to find jobs.

Berti knew that Albania couldn't afford to lose their young people and so the church came up with the idea of starting a school. It would serve the local church, employ Christians, giving them an incentive to stay in the country, and teach young people to learn English, which would provide them with a better chance of finding work. It would also give the church respect and a good reputation within the community.

With the help of ECM workers Stephen Bell, Murray Cotter and Douglas Livingston, Albanian Christians started English classes in Lushnje, Fier and Patos, calling them Victory Schools. They appointed a board in each of the three towns so the classes could be run professionally, fulfil all legal requirements, and most importantly, would be recognised by the Albanian authorities.

The first class began in Fier in September 1997 with eight students. A month later another started in Lushnje after a believer allowed the second floor of her two-storey house to be used. At the first lesson were five pupils, who paid 10 American dollars a month.

ECM provided a TV, video, tables and desks, while the Abraham Lincoln Foundation of Albania gave books, equipment and other educational material, as well as advising on how to set up and run the school.

"Although I had no experience in managing a school, I did not see it as a business, but as a service to God," said Berti. "I work for the school and God grows it."

And the school has certainly grown. It was a credit to Berti's character that he was flexible and willing to have a go at a completely new project.

Within a year, it expanded with three teachers using all three rooms on the second floor and teaching nine hour-long classes, each with a maximum of up to ten pupils.

As further premises were needed, one of the Christian teachers, Elsa Ndrecka, mentioned she was friends with a girl whose family lived in a large house 200 metres away from the classrooms. The family invited Berti and Elsa to look round the house. As they climbed the stairs to the third floor of the large building, Berti turned to Elsa and said: "One day all this will be ours."

He was correct, the building became the Victory School, but it would be another ten years before his prophecy came true.

The father, Loni, let them rent two rooms to provide a fourth and fifth classroom.

Many Albanians were desperate to learn English, and through Berti's leadership skills and the school's growing reputation for high standards and honesty – he insisted the school paid all its high taxes in full – numbers grew every year.

All the students were prepared for Level 1 and Level 2 Examinations and those who passed were presented with a certificate from the Lincoln Foundation, which was recognised by the Albanian Ministry of Employment.

By 2000, the school employed their fifth teacher, Alma Syla, who had certainly come into the profession the hard way.

When many Albanians left the country in 1990, attracted by better-paid jobs abroad, there were many job vacancies in professions, including teaching.

Eighteen-year-old Alma had wanted to be a teacher since she was a child and she decided to apply, even though she hadn't any qualifications.

To her delight, she was offered a job, but it was in a remote village. To get to the school in Spolet, it meant catching the 6.30am bus from Lushnje for an hour's journey before a 45-minute walk through two villages to the school, where she started teaching at 8.30am and finished at 1.30pm. Then she had to repeat the journey, arriving home at 3pm.

After a meal and a rest, she started her own studies and preparing the next day's lessons, until 10.30pm, depending on whether there were any power cuts, which were frequent then.

Alma tried for a scholarship to study part-time at a university in Tirana. Although a few thousand students had applied, Alma was one of only 100 selected, and in the autumn of 1990, she began a diploma in Albanian language and literature.

Soon after she started, the students went on strike on December 8, 1990; the Government responded by closing the universities and didn't re-open them until the following April. This affected Alma's studies and impacted on Berti who was ordered to join the Rapid Defence Force in Kavaja to deal with the civil unrest. Meanwhile, Alma had to concentrate on her teaching and had to put back her studies for a term, as she couldn't take her exams because the university was shut.

In 1991, Alma moved to a school nearer her home in Lushnje. Fier-Seman was only an hour's bus ride away, and no walk at the other end. However, over the next few years, life became even more hectic as she continued her teaching and her studies in the evening.

In 1994, she married Drini, who ran his own electrical business in Lushnje, and the following year she gave birth to her first daughter, Sabrina. As if that was not enough, in June she started to learn English at a neighbour's house. Their 20-year-old daughter, Enkeleda, taught Alma English while Alma's mother looked after Sabrina.

"Enkeleda was very hard-working but very poor," recalled Alma, "but she was so happy and always singing.

"When I asked her why she was always singing, she said it was because she was a Christian."

It started many discussions between Enkeleda and Alma during the English conversation classes and led to them eventually praying together with Enkeleda's mother.

"That was the start of my Christian journey," said Alma.

At the same time, Alma became very friendly with Elsa, a Christian teacher at her school.

They began sitting together on the bus and spent the hour's journey in prayer and studying the Bible together. Elsa gave Alma her first Bible, which she still uses today.

The pair taught at a school for 14-18-year-old pupils, where most of the villagers were from an Orthodox background. However, when the two teachers spoke about their faith to the students, the director called them into his office and banned them from talking about religion.

Even so, the students wanted to continue the discussions and one of the parents let them use his dusty old office in a little used house in the village.

Alma and Elsa accepted his offer, cleaned and painted the room and brought in bricks and wood to provide benches.

Every Thursday at 2pm, after school had finished, the two teachers went to their new office and taught Christianity for an hour.

"We had up to 60 students," said Alma, "and though the parents knew what was going on, they didn't mind and even welcomed us into their homes."

After two years, Elsa moved to another job. "I cried on the bus when I heard the news," said Alma, who continued at that school for two years before getting a job in Lushnje. She worked there in the morning, and in 2000 started teaching at the Victory School in the afternoons, where numbers were then more than 100.

To cope with the increasing numbers, Berti again went to the owner, Loni, to ask for more rooms. Loni happily agreed to rent the school another three rooms because there was now only him and his wife left at home, as their two daughters and son had emigrated to America.

By 2004, Loni and his wife decided to join their children in the States and they told Berti: "The building is all yours."

He allowed them to rent the whole building and develop it as they wished for 600 American dollars a month, and Berti, with his amazing vision and ability to plan ahead, set about finding the money to allow the church to buy the property. Three years later the building was bought for 210,000 American dollars, with the money raised from school profits, donations and a large loan from ECM.

In the meantime, with the help of builders and church volunteers, they added a second floor to provide three more classrooms so they could move the school to one site. Even after this, the small church still had the vision for further projects.

Finding a job was still a problem for the students, so in 2004 they began two new ventures.

First, they introduced two IT classes five times a week. Berti persuaded Charles Bell, from Calvary Church in California, USA, to help them by sending teams to Lushnje to teach English and IT studies, as well as providing cash, laptops, digital projectors and advice on training.

Secondly, when the charity Hope for Albania, a Christian relief agency based in the Netherlands, provided Berti with six sewing machines, they decided to start a tailoring class, to help women find work and start businesses.

They set aside a room in the school to provide free two-hour lessons twice a week for a three-month course. It proved a great success and more than 60 women completed the training and many joined the church, including Alma's mother, Ervehe Tabaku.

The school was aware that many children could not afford to come, so they introduced a scholarship scheme and many from poor backgrounds took advantage of it.

Berti said there were many joys in running both the school and the church. One of those was to see students organising shows, concerts and celebrations in the church, which would attract their parents and friends.

"The church became known in the community because of the growing reputation of the Victory School," said Berti.

However, there were frustrations as well. "One of those was living in a town where the young people go away at 18, either to university or abroad, and few return," said Berti. "Because of that we are always looking for new leaders in the church and new teachers in the school."

Berti knew that from personal experience as both his daughter, Alta, and his son, Dorian, went away to university.

When Alta began to learn English at school, she helped Berti to prepare and translate the Sunday school material. As she got older, she started taking the classes on her own and then translating Biblical commentaries to help her father with his sermons. When there was an English-speaking preacher in church, Alta was the translator. Later she led the teenage Bible study in church. Then she accompanied Berti when he travelled abroad, as he told churches about the work in Albania.

"She became my right hand, she was superb," said Berti.

Alta also helped Berti at the Victory School. When Alta went to university in 2001 to study English and become a teacher, she still supported the school and the church work when she came home.

Unlike many youngsters, Alta did come back to Lushnje and helped more with the school management. When she married Lenci, Berti was so impressed with his new son-in-law that he appointed him assistant pastor at the church and course director at the Victory School; jobs he did for five years.

He said: "I am very grateful to God for giving me Alta and Lenci, they have been great supporters in my ministry and my life and I was thrilled when they were the first couple to be married at the Way of Peace Church on September 11, 2005."

Another great helper was Berti's son, Dorian, who has been going to the church since he was five years old.

"He is an IT specialist and God has used his gift for the Way of Peace Church and the Victory School," said Berti.

Even when Dorian went to university in Tirana to study computer sciences, he came home many weekends to check the IT systems in the church and the school.

Berti could never solve the drain of young people completely, although the Victory School also helped some to get local employment. Two of the pupils, Ingrida Nako and Erisa Xhaja, who had learnt English at the school, both returned to teach there.

Berti never allowed anything to faze him as he was totally committed to do what God wanted. Still, it was quite an achievement for a former electrician and kiosk owner to open a school and take on the financial responsibility of running it without any training, as well as overseeing a church at the same time.

However, the church was quite a way from the school so Berti was always travelling between the two. Berti knew he could solve the problem of being in different places as pastor and school principal, but it was another ambitious and costly scheme, which he would put shortly to both the church and the school.

21

COPING WITH HALF A MILLION REFUGEES

After the baptism of fire with the pyramid selling scandal in 1997, the young Albanian church might have thought things would calm down. But within months, the church faced a different, but just as serious challenge, when more than half a million refugees, the equivalent to 15 per cent of Albania's population, fled into the country from the war in Kosovo in late 1998 and early 1999.

The Kosovo question had been a problem throughout Albania's history. Following the First Balkan War of 1912, the Treaty of London recognised Kosovo as part of Serbia, which later became Yugoslavia. It also recognised Albania as an independent sovereign state, even though more than half the Albanian population were left outside the new state's borders.

Under President Tito, Kosovo was practically self-governing by 1974. But tensions increased in the 1980s with the Kosovo Albanians wanting to become a republic within Yugoslavia while the Kosovo Serbs wanted closer ties with Serbia.

By August 1987, Kosovo Serbs felt the Communist authorities in Belgrade were neglecting them, and when a rising politician, Slobodan Milosevic, arrived in Kosovo and appealed to Serb nationalism, he was treated as a hero. Following the end of Communism, relations between the two communities deteriorated further as the Serbians took control and many Albanians lost their jobs. Then thousands of Serb refugees from Croatia settled in Kosovo in 1995.

By late 1997, the situation escalated into war with many Kosovo Albanians killed. Many others were forced from their homes at gunpoint, with most of them fleeing over the border into Albania.

The Albanian Foreign Ministry called for NATO military intervention to stop the fighting and eventually all sides were invited to an international conference in Rambouillet, France, in February 1999. Following the breakdown of talks, NATO forces launched a bombing campaign against Yugoslavia from March 24 until June 10 to force Milosevic back to the negotiating table and to withdraw his forces from Kosovo.[17]

---

17 *Blue Guide: Albania & Kosovo* by James Pettifer.

With half a million refugees streaming into the country, Albania's fragile infrastructure collapsed, leaving their government and the international humanitarian agencies unable to cope.

However, help arrived from an unexpected quarter. The Albanian Evangelical Alliance (the Vëllazëria Ungjillore e Shqipërise or VUSh in Albanian) stepped in. It had been set up in October 1993 as an umbrella organisation for the evangelical churches and drew inspiration from an evangelical brotherhood founded in 1892 by Gjerasim Qiraiazi to unite the people to work for the good of the nation.

With a network of 120 churches across the country, VUSh volunteered to organise and run transit centres in every major town and city.

At the time, its president was Berti, who had been appointed in October 1997 for three years in office.

"When I was at the Albanian Bible Institute members of VUSh came to meet me," recalled Berti, "and said many people had recommended me to be the next VUSh president."

He added: "I was speechless for a few moments, but as I am a person who enjoys a challenge, I immediately thought it was God's plan for me to contribute to the Albanian church and I accepted it. I was honoured and felt very privileged."

As well as meetings in Albania, Berti represented the country abroad at Balkan, European and World conferences, and he went to Amsterdam for a Billy Graham conference in 2000.

"It gave me the opportunity to say what God was doing in Albania, that the new churches were starting to grow and that the country was now open as a mission field," said Berti.

However, within 18 months of Berti taking office, he and VUSh were in the national spotlight because of the Kosovo crisis.

"We were totally unprepared for this and we had no experience in dealing with it," he said. "It was a very difficult role for me as I had two duties. In Tirana, as VUSh president, I had to manage the situation for the evangelical Albanian churches while in Lushnje, as a pastor, I had to oversee the situation there. It was like a war on two fronts."

They dealt with the situation in four ways. Firstly, in Tirana the executive committee of VUSh organised an emergency meeting, where they fasted and prayed. Secondly, they set up a headquarters to manage the situation and contacted all the churches offering them VUSh's support and asking them what their needs were. Thirdly, they launched a website to communicate with all the churches and tell them what was going on. Fourthly, they sent an SOS to churches and organisations abroad asking them to help with prayer, money and emergency supplies.

In Lushnje, Berti, like many pastors, challenged their church by asking members: "Are you ready to help our brothers and sisters in need?"

They were, and they rose to the challenge brilliantly.

More than 5,000 refugees came to Lushnje in March 1999. The first wave was people coming to stay with relatives. All the churches in the town responded, giving their own food and blankets, before the international aid arrived, including financial help from ECM.

Alma and her husband, Drini, whose parents are Kosovans, lived in a small rented two-roomed flat with their two children. When Drini's relatives arrived, they stored all the furniture in one room, while 12 of them lived in the other one.

"Each morning we piled up all the mattresses on the one bed to make room for us all," recalled Alma.

There was no bathroom nor running water in their sixth-floor flat. For water, they had to go down to the tap on the ground floor and carry it back up six flights of stairs. For a bath, they had again to go down to the ground floor, cross the street and up to the fourth floor of a block of flats nearby to use the bathroom at Alma's parents' house.

"Despite 12 of us living so close together, none of us got any infections," said Alma.

In the second wave, refugees without relatives in Lushnje came into the town camping on the sides of the roads and local people took complete strangers into their homes. Even though many of the Lushnje people were very poor, and were still recovering from losing their money in the pyramid scandal, they gave so much to help the refugees.

Civic officials in Lushnje called a Council of Emergency and invited all the institutions, organisations and churches to decide how to pool their resources.

A new board was set up for the town with Berti representing the six evangelical churches. With his military, emergency planning and organisational skills, he was the ideal candidate and he immediately submitted a plan of action, on behalf of the churches, to the Council of Emergency.

The board decided to divide Lushnja up into zones, with the churches looking after one zone.

Berti arranged to rent four shops, paid for by the churches and staffed by local Christians, to provide free bread for the refugees. The board also hired a depot to store all the international aid coming into Lushnje. However, within three weeks, they had to find another depot as it was too small.

In Tirana, Gani, Adile, and their four children, who were all Kosovo Albanians, had 30 relatives staying in their two-bedroom house for a time.

"When the relatives returned to Kosovo the house seemed quite large with just five of us in," he joked.

Further south in Albania, Stephen wrote: "We alone in Fier (pop 70,000) have more than 12,000 refugees.

"The four evangelical churches in Fier have united in their efforts to distribute aid and love to these poor people. We started with £300, which we collected among ourselves, and are now expecting generous gifts from British, French, German and American Christians. They have sent money and trucks, which should begin to arrive next week. We have bought clothes and food for about 1,000 Kosovans who are living in 'institutions.' These are the fourth and fifth floors of the officers' houses, where 242 people are living on one floor under our rented meeting hall.

"I have also visited 160 people where three large families are living in an open barn, about the size of a five-a-side football pitch. The family of Ibrahim, a very good friend of Shau-Ping, my Chinese Christian friend in my Prishtina days, had to travel for five days in an open lorry with 70 others, passing beheaded corpses on the roadside.

"Trying to get them accommodation in Fier, was a soul-destroying task. On the one hand, there are Albanians who want £220 a month rent from a family of eight. On the other hand, there is a couple in Fier with three children who are living in the reception area of a disused and derelict cinema, and they are willing to move up to a windowless attic to allow these poor Kosovans to move into their space. Truly, this mess brings out the best and the worst in people."

One of those sent out by ECM to help the churches in May 1999 was Arthur Prescott, whose business skills proved invaluable as he looked after the warehouse in Fier.

"Stephen Bell and the local Christians, including Berti in Lushnje, had done such a great job that many of the larger professional aid agencies were envious of what had already been achieved before they arrived," said Arthur.

"But even they were overwhelmed with the money, food and clothes flooding in from the West.

"When I arrived in Fier, Stephen gave me several large bags full of currencies from all over the world and asked me to get them changed into Albanian lek (the local currency) which was quite a challenge since there were no operating banks. All money had to be changed using one of the many money changers in the town square – their sleight of hand was something to be admired."

On June 10, 1999, the war ended with the Kumanovo agreement, which agreed to transfer the governing of Kosovo to the United Nations.

Next day, a NATO-led Kosovo Force entered the area to provide security to the UN Mission in Kosovo.

After 78 days of war, about half of the 200,000 Kosovo Serbs left Kosovo in the summer of 1999, while the ethnic Albanians, ignoring UN warnings of danger, returned to their homes in Kosovo.

There was a huge line of traffic as the grateful Kosovo Albanians headed home on whatever transport they could find, ranging from cars, lorries, tractors and any agricultural vehicle that could move.

As the Christians still had some money and goods left over once the refugees had returned home, Arthur and Stephen decided to hire a lorry, fill it with the remaining food and clothes, plus fridges and cookers, and return with the refugees to Kosovo.

With a local driver and a translator, Arthur began the 10-hour journey from Fier in southern Albania to Peja in Kosovo over the mountain passes.

"With no signposts and many obstacles, it was a treacherous and hairy trip – but quite an adventure," said Arthur, who went to Peja because they had contacts there through Gani's family. When they arrived, they were shocked by what greeted them.

The streets were in total darkness and many of the buildings owned by Kosovo Albanians were destroyed, while nearby were the smouldering homes of Serbians, who had fled as the Kosovo Albanians returned home.

"Whole streets were full of rubble three feet high and it was very difficult to get around," said Arthur. "The Serbians had first shelled the civilian homes and businesses, and then had gone down the streets firebombing every Kosovo Albanian house, which had collapsed inwardly, so they were just piles of rubble as well. On top of that the Italian peace-keeping troops warned about mines and firebombs that hadn't been detonated."

Arthur spent two weeks there, delivering the goods, talking to the UN and aid agencies, filming and planning his next trip. He returned a few months later when

ECM launched a long-term project to help rebuild homes and support families in Peja, Prishtina and nearby villages.

"The people were just in despair, we had to help," said Arthur.

Berti said that according to VUSh's own statistics, during the first two weeks of the crisis, the evangelicals, who total fewer than half a per cent of the population, dealt with nearly 80 per cent of the refugees. They ensured they were met, fed, registered and sent out to families or camps to be looked after.

"We are still amazed what God did through His churches in Albania," said Berti. "It was a big test of the church and they coped well. A lot of friendships were made and some became Christians."

After the crisis was over President Rexhep Mejdani said: "I wish to acknowledge the Evangelical believers of Albania for the dedication and service rendered to tens of thousands of refugees during one of the most difficult chapters in the history of our nation. Throughout the country these believers exemplified faith in action through their practical application of the Golden Rule, 'Do unto others as you would have them do unto you'."

Praise from the Albanian president for its work was a turning point for the church.

Just over 30 years ago, a previous president, Enver Hoxha, said there was no God and closed all the churches.

22

I WILL BUILD MY CHURCH

(Matthew 16 verse 18)

It was in early 1998 that Berti decided the church had to look for new premises. There was no point in going back to the dental building where they had had the problems with the armed raid and other thefts.

For the last few months, they had been meeting in a believer's apartment, but it was very cramped and Berti decided it was only fair that the church should move.

It was Berti's friend Ladi, and ECM Eastern Europe director Stuart Rowell, who came up with an unusual solution.

In Albania it is traditional that, when a son gets married, his parents give him land to build a house. So Ladi, who had married in 1987, had built a two-storey house, which included a large flat roof and balcony, on his parents' land next to his and Berti's kiosk.

Stuart, who had trained as a construction engineer before joining ECM, suggested rather ingeniously, putting a roof over the flat area and Ladi could rent that part of his house out to the church, to which he agreed.

While they were planning the Balcony Church as the believers called it, Stephen Bell came to preach at the Way of Peace Church and took as his theme the Old Testament Book of Nehemiah. There, the prophet had challenged the Jews to rebuild in 52 days the walls of Jerusalem, which were in a desolate state after King Nebuchadnezzar had destroyed the city and taken most of the Jews into exile in the 6th century BC.

Berti then called on the Lushnje Christians to build their church on the balcony in 52 days – and they rose to the challenge.

ECM loaned the church 5,000 American dollars and together with other donations, they began building in May. A church in Tirana had a business producing corrugated iron and Berti negotiated a good price for the roof material. Ladi had a friend, Agim, who was a professional builder and he agreed to oversee the project. Every church member gave of his or her time and talents. Berti did the electrics, while some of the teenagers went to school in the morning and spent their afternoons labouring on the balcony. Meanwhile, other young people in the church formed a long line to pass the bricks and cement up to the builders on the balcony. By June 1, the

Balcony Church was completed, 52 days after the project was launched.

"It was a great team effort and I was really grateful for all their help," said Berti.

Stuart Rowell added: "I was really impressed by Berti. His organisational skills are phenomenal. He is always working on a plethora of activities and he gets people working. He has a large vision and has an ability to persevere, even with limited resources as this project showed."

On Sunday, June 7, 1998, the church celebrated with its first service in the new building.

At the same time, Berti completed his three-year course at the Albanian Bible Institute and Stephen suggested that he became both the full-time pastor and principal of the school.

Berti knew it would be difficult financially, if he gave up his job as the notary's assistant. In addition, he didn't receive a pension from the army, as he had completed only 11 years' military service, not the minimum 15 years.

But the church was growing and Berti decided to talk to the members about having a full-time pastor.

The church agreed that they wanted a full-time pastor, and that it should be Berti.

In the autumn, Berti resigned as a notary's assistant and sold his share in the kiosk business, although Ladi kindly gave him a third of the kiosk profits for the next two years to help him financially. He also returned the capital that Berti had put into the business.

Now he had the kiosk money, Berti decided he wouldn't take a salary as pastor, as he was already taking one as principal of the Victory School.

On Sunday, October 4, 1998, more than 100 people packed into the Balcony Church to see Berti appointed pastor.

"It was a very emotional moment," said Berti. "Although I was excited, I was also a little fearful of the future. It was a big challenge and I was concerned whether I would be a good pastor."

However, as well as the joys, there were also a few difficulties for Berti. One of them was trying to get more men to come to the church.

Berti believes this reticence is down to the role of men in Albanian society who are the head of the family. Men are expected to obey their parents and accept their way of life, including religion. Men are responsible if any member followed a different course to their ancestors' traditions, such as becoming a Christian.

In addition, he said, men could not afford to lose face with friends or family, and going to church would be considered odd. Berti knew that Albanian men have an inner personal pride that stopped them committing themselves to any religion that was new to them. Another problem was that some, who came from an Orthodox background, said they were Christians, even though they never went to church.

To try to meet the men, Berti often used to go out to the cafes, where he would spend the evening chatting to other men over a Turkish coffee.

As a result, some men were attracted to the church, and within five years, the Balcony Church had doubled from 30 to more than 60 people meaning that the building was now too small.

Berti began to make plans to build a new church at the back of the Victory School. Again, the church didn't have much money, so they decided to do the project in stages. Firstly, they planned to clear the area, secondly to put down a floor and finally to build the roof and the walls.

The owner, who was about to emigrate to America, allowed the church members to clear the garden area and get the site ready.

For the next few months, they continued to meet at the Balcony Church and it wasn't until April 2004 that they had enough money to pay for the floor; a job they decided had to be done by professionals.

They celebrated the completion of the new floor with a special show by the school students to which friends and family were invited.

However, in the middle of the show, the heavens opened and they had to move hurriedly inside and complete it in the school.

Now they knew that they had to put a roof on as quickly as possible. To help the financial situation Berti and the board split the church and the school into two separate entities, with the church owning the site and the school paying them rent. At the same time, Hope for Albania gave them some roofing materials, which galvanised them into action.

Again, members decided to build the church themselves. With help from Agim the builder, Berti the electrician and the church volunteers, mixing concrete and cement, they started building at Easter 2005. It was finished a couple of months later in June.

The roof materials of the Balcony Church, which were not suitable for the new church, were given away, so allowing Ladi to incorporate the second storey into his home.

Life became more hectic for Berti, so in November 2006, Tatjana quit her job at the court to spend more time in the church helping Berti.

Then on July 27, 2008, a packed Way of Peace Church celebrated its 15th anniversary with representatives from churches in Lushnje, Tirana and other Way of Peace churches, plus the Albanian Evangelical Alliance and Hope for Albania.

The service gave Berti the chance to remind the congregation of all that had been achieved since the church began in 1993.

"It was a joyous day," said Berti. "I told them what God had done through using ordinary people in an extraordinary way.

"The results were amazing," he continued. "We had succeeded in bringing Christianity to the people in a practical way. With the aid of generous organisations, such as Hope for Albania, we had been able to help many people in the town and in the villages.

"We had helped the disabled, the homeless, the poor, the widows and the orphans. We had shown everyone that God cares for the helpless and He does that through his own people, the church."

An important feature of that anniversary service was the ordination of Sokol Kertusha, as the new pastor of a church in Durres, which the Way of Peace Church in Lushnje had re-started in 2006. Every Sunday afternoon for the last year, Berti had made the two-hour round trip to Emmanuel Church, Durres, to lead the service, to preach and to help train Sokol.

During the anniversary service, the congregation prayed for Berti recognising him as their full-time pastor and to carry on the work in Durres that, by tradition, was started there 2,000 years ago, by the Apostle Paul himself.

23

BEHIND EVERY DOOR THERE'S A STORY

As a trainee journalist, I was told: "Behind every door there's a story, and if you talk to a person long enough, you will find it." That is certainly true of the Way of Peace Church in Lushnje, where probably every one of the 70 members has a fascinating tale about their journey to faith. However, there is only room here for three of them.

Servete Cani, born in 1946 in Lushnje, was the only daughter of a very poor family. She had three brothers, but their father died when they were very young. Their father's sister, who had six older children of her own, helped look after her three nephews and a niece, while Servete's mother worked and eventually remarried. Incidentally, one of those six cousins is Vace Zela who became one of Albania's top singers with an international reputation.

To help the family finances, Servete left school at 14 and found a job as a tailor's assistant at the factory where Ladi's father, Leksi, was the manager. She worked there for 29 years, until it was closed in 1990 as the country moved from being a Communist to a Capitalist state. Leksi told Berti that Servete, who had two sons by an arranged marriage, was a model worker. On top of that, Servete, who learnt business studies in the evening, was so hard working and trustworthy that he 'could have given her the keys to the factory and nothing would have been touched or taken'.

One of her nieces was Alma Syla, who explained the Christian message to her and invited her to the Way of Peace Church.

Servete recalled: "I felt so welcomed by the church and was particularly impressed by Berti, who even though he was talking to a group of friends, saw me and came over to me."

A little later, her husband Zyberi, who worked for a group helping disabled people, also visited the church. Berti met him when he talked to Zyberi's group after the church had been given some wheelchairs. They both became committed members of the church and Servete was a deacon for a number of years.

(Since the first edition of this book was published in 2010 Zyberi has since died.)

Bedrija Manaj, the youngest of five children, had a tough start to life. In 1943, when she was only 12 months old, her father, a farmer, was killed by a German bomb while walking along the road. Soon afterwards, her mother heard that the Germans and the Albanian collaborators, the Ballists, were closing in on her village, Sevaster, near Vlorë. She knew she couldn't escape from the village with five youngsters, so to protect Bedrija, she wrapped her in a blanket and hid her in the bough of a nearby tree. The Germans marched straight through the village, but the Ballists stopped and explained to the villagers that they were fighting for the future of Albania – and promptly stole some of their sheep, goats and produce. Fortunately, they didn't harm anyone. Bedrija's mother later told her that God had protected her because she had not cried out during the three hours when the soldiers had been in the village.

Bedrija went to school in the morning and helped her mother in the afternoon working the land. This continued until she was 13 when her family told her they had chosen her bridegroom. A few days later, his family came over to drink coffee with Bedrija's family and proposed a toast, wishing the couple future happiness.

However, there was one person missing. They came without the future bridegroom, so Bedrija didn't meet

Resul until he got out of the car on their wedding day, August 28, 1958, which was a few weeks before her 16th birthday.

Bedrija said, for both families, it was important that the boy and girl had had a good upbringing, not whether they were attracted to one another.

Compared to previous generations Bedrija was a slow starter. Her mother was married when she was 12 years old and her grandmother when she was 13. As both wore veils on their wedding days, their future bridegrooms had no idea what their brides looked like until they took their veils off in the bedroom after the ceremony.

Bedrija said she learnt to love her husband, Resul, who had respected her throughout her life – and they have now been happily married for more than 60 years.

After the wedding, Bedrija joined her husband in Lushnje, where she spent 15 years selling food at a state shop in the day, and studying at night. The couple had four children and Bedrija later became an economist in the government forestry department, retiring in 1996.

She started coming to church after her eldest daughter had married a Christian, and a neighbour had invited Bedrija's granddaughter to Sunday school. Bedrija went along to see her granddaughter and became a church member.

She helps at the prayer meeting now. Every day she gets up at 6am, spends an hour in prayer, then two hours in Bible study, followed by another hour of prayer in the afternoon and 15 minutes in prayer at night before she goes to sleep. She writes a daily page in her large diary of her prayer requests and folds the page over when they have been answered. She is now on volume four of her prayer diaries – and there are very few pages that haven't been folded over.

Vera Pirra, who was born in 1959 in the village of Petove, near Fier, didn't complete her schooling until she was 25 years old. She had had to leave school early and find a job to provide money for her parents and her two brothers and a sister. For six years, she worked in a vegetable packing factory, but then her family allowed her to go back to school to take business studies. At the end of her first year, her three friends all failed to make it into the second year. As it was some distance away, her father, a nurse at the village clinic, wouldn't let Vera go on her own, so she had to leave.

When she visited her cousin, who worked at a flour factory in Lushnje, he introduced her to one of his friends. A year later they were married and Vera moved into her in-laws' two-bedroom home. She soon had a son, Mikel, and when he was seven months old, Vera became pregnant again. Her husband said they were so poor she would have to have an abortion. When Vera refused, he told her: "Choose me or the baby." She chose the baby.

The couple divorced and Vera returned to her village home in Petove where her family supported her and her two children for the next two years.

In Enver Hoxha's time, the law said that a mother had the right to a home in the baby's town of birth, even if she was divorced.

Vera wanted to return to Lushnje with her two children. However, her father decided it wasn't safe for her to go on her own, so he went with her and stayed for six months, before going back to his wife in Petove.

Another of Vera's cousins introduced her to Banush, a mechanic, who was widowed with a daughter and a son. She felt sorry for him and allowed him to share her house. However, as living together was frowned upon in Albania, they married in 1989 and later had a daughter Greta.

One of the believers at the Way of Peace Church invited Greta to the Sunday school and Vera decided to go as well.

She found the church very welcoming and, as she went along to meetings, prayed and read the Bible, she found the answers to her questions such as 'Who is God?' and 'How can I find Him?'

Vera, who worked selling goods from a street stall and then as a hospital cleaner, became a deacon at the church.

Her husband, who had changed jobs from working as a mechanic to working in a water irrigation firm, also started coming to church occasionally. But he was diagnosed with Parkinson's disease in 2000 and now finds it too difficult to attend.

That wasn't the end of illness problems for the family. In 2006, 15-year-old Greta was diagnosed with scoliosis, an abnormal curvature of the spine, and was in danger of being crippled for life. Vera, accompanied by Berti and Tatjana, travelled with Greta to a specialist in Macedonia. After two years, there seemed no improvement and then they heard of a Greek professor in Tirana who would operate at a cost of 8,000 Euros. The church launched an appeal and, with the help of ECM, Hope for Albania and church members, they raised the money. Again, Berti and Tatjana went with Vera and Greta to Tirana, and ten days later, they returned home with Greta after the operation.

"Now Greta is walking totally normally, it really was a great answer to prayer," said Berti.

(Since the first edition of this book was published in 2010 Vera has since died.)

24

LET YOUR LIGHT SHINE . . .

"Let your light shine before men that they may see your good deeds and praise your Father in heaven," says Jesus in Matthew's Gospel, chapter 5 verse 16.

The church in Lushnje takes Jesus' words and its social responsibility very seriously. Once the church was built, the congregation could concentrate on other projects, besides the Victory School, to help the community.

"We want to be known by the community and for them to know who we are, so we can help them," said Berti. "We start with families, then move on to their friends, going out into the neighbourhoods, before expanding into the towns and further into the villages."

Some of these projects were more unusual, but very practical.

In 2007, local youngsters thought it was great fun to use the streetlights in the road outside the church and Victory School as target practice with their catapults. The problem was that it gets dark by 4pm in Lushnje in the winter, making it unsafe for both the older and younger worshippers to come to church and school events. After discussing the problem, members decided to send Berti to the local government offices to offer them 500 American dollars to buy some new street light bulbs with metal meshes to protect them.

They accepted Berti's offer and carried out the work. "We got lots of thanks from the neighbourhood, for what was quite a small but very effective project," said Berti.

As the church grew, it became more involved in social work in Lushnje itself. When the hospital was short of basic equipment, they helped raise money for beds, mattresses and even surgical gloves and uniforms, through members and Hope for Albania. The charity provided gifts, which church members translated into Boxes of Joy, to give to patients when they visited the hospital. They also received from abroad shoeboxes containing sweets, pens, pencils and shampoos, and handed them out to local children. These are now so popular that they have become annual events.

However, it wasn't only in Lushnje that the church began to help their local community. In the nearby villages, the church launched two of its most ambitious projects – building two homes for poor families and restoring a school.

In the West, the homes where the families were living in Barbullinje and Bitaj, would have been condemned as unfit for human habitation. On top of that, the children of Myzafer Cili's family in Barbullinje had never even been to school. However, although the tumbledown shacks were health risks, the families, including their young children, lived there for years, until Berti and a church team arrived. Berti contacted Hope for Albania, who provided craftsmen and materials and rebuilt the homes within six months. Now church members visit the families every month bringing food parcels for them and other poor families.

"It was great to see the joy on the families' faces when they moved into their new homes," said Berti.

One of the biggest projects the church was involved in was rebuilding the school at Gramsh, a very old and unsafe primary and secondary school, with 320 children from the ages of 6 to 15, plus 20 teachers.

At the same time as the church was thinking about work in the villages, officials from Hope for Albania approached Berti and said they had funds to restore a school and wanted to link up with them. Berti went to the Educational Department in Lushnje, who gave him the names of three schools which were in desperate need of support, including the one at Gramsh.

After praying, the church and Hope for Albania decided to help the school at Gramsh, which is seven kilometres from Lushnje. They went to meet the chairman of the village commune, the school director, teachers and students, who told them the school had been successful for many years. Then the building began to fall into disrepair and they couldn't afford the repairs.

"We took photographs of the school as we realised that the situation was appalling," said Berti. "The ceiling of the second floor was leaking and damaged in many places. They had abandoned the second floor, as it was dangerous to put children in the classes there.

"We knew that investing in the school was investing in the future of Albania," said Berti, who agreed to the project.

In the summer of June 2008, while the pupils were on holiday, the charity brought in a construction company, who did the majority of the restoration work. Members of Berti's church and students at the school carried out some of the minor jobs, including giving the whole school a major clean-up afterwards.

The building work was finished in the September, in time for the new term. The villagers held a celebration and inauguration ceremony on September 25 where Berti explained why, as Christians, they wanted to help the school. Afterwards, much to Berti's surprise, he was called on to the stage and was presented with a certificate making him an Honorary Citizen of Gramsh.

Berti added: "I was delighted and very touched with the award. It showed that the villagers were very thankful for our help with the project, which has transformed the school. It also showed to everyone that we keep our promises."

He said they would like to plant a church in Gramsh one day. However, in the meantime, they have continued to support the school by providing new equipment such as stoves, desks, chairs, blackboards and sports equipment. With ECM's help, the church has supported 19 poor families with food and clothing.

However, it wasn't only in Lushnje and nearby villages that the church were involved. At the end of July 2009, members of the church went on a mission to Kosovo to support Gani who was now running a church in Peja by joining an international team. While the men and women went visiting in Peja and the nearby villages of Kyushu and Radovan, the boys played football with local teenagers and the girls helped with painting and cleaning at the school during the day and baby-sat in the evenings so parents could attend the meetings.

Berti said: "It was an enjoyable week, we built links with the church in Kosovo and the members of our church learnt much."

Another important ministry for the church was providing wheelchairs for the disabled, because in Albania there is little state help, and many disabled people never even leave their homes.

When Berti was given 200 wheelchairs by Hope for Albania in October 2007, he was left with a problem. He didn't know how to distribute that many, so he advertised on the two TV stations, offering them free to families who called him. As they came to the church, Berti gave them the wheelchairs and then offered them free English and computer courses at the Victory School as well. After nine students completed the course seven months later, they held a big award ceremony in the church to which town officials, including the director of the employment office, as well as friends and family, came.

"One of the aims was to give the disabled a chance to integrate into our society," said Berti. "By learning to use a computer and to speak English they have a better opportunity to find work, which is very hard in Albania."

To help disabled people further, Alma, who taught at a state school in the morning and in the afternoon at the Victory School, linked up with one of the town schools.

"We wanted to make children aware that these people are part of society, even though they have been hidden away for years and years," she added. "They also need our love, our care and our support."

Many had been impressed by the church's efforts over the years, including Dr Janet Goodall and Mervyn Kirkpatrick, a social worker with the Causeway Trust in Northern Ireland.

Dr Goodall said: "Few people bothered about the disabled in Albania. So, when Berti and his church became involved, it was a huge step forward in that country and showed the caring side of the pastor and the church."

In July 2005, Mervyn had joined an ECM team visiting Lushnje and he was so moved that he decided to spend part of his retirement helping them.

"During our time preparing for the church project, we were able to locate in the country only one facility for mental health, one school for children with learning disabilities and one facility for physical disabilities," he said after his visit.

Mervyn decided to launch a day care centre in partnership with the church and, in June 2008, they began a pilot two-week project.

Berti, whose church had been preparing for this event for a year, said: "We aimed to help people with mental and physical disabilities, to show them Christ's love, as well as to awake in the patients and their family members, the hope of change in their way of living."

The team consisted of seven individuals from various churches in Northern Ireland, including a physiotherapist, two occupational therapists, a social worker, a music therapist and two youth workers. Fourteen members of the Lushnje church were trained to work alongside the Irish team.

Along with the local church volunteers, the team set up a day care facility in the church for the 17 children and adults. The programme, called Way of Hope, consisted of arts and crafts, sports and games, music, refreshments and ended with massage and relaxation exercises.

"Throughout our time with the young people and their carers we could see an improvement in their confidence and social skills," said Mervyn. "Many of them learned new skills and tried new things, such as music, games and crafts."

He said the carers were challenged by the project as they saw how their children developed in such a short time, and how they interacted with the other young people and the adults.

Berti added: "The families were also hugely impacted by the project. Experiencing our love, acceptance, care and friendliness, the parents saw how their children played with others, and it was wonderful to hear them worship God and being open to following Jesus Christ."

Some of the families started attending church because they had seen how loved and accepted their children were.

Two people who really enjoyed the project were Blerim and Taulant.

Blerim is in his early 20s and has epileptic fits three or four times a day. He was not accepted at school, so had to stay at home with only his family for company and was not used to socialising.

Mervyn said: "During his two weeks at the centre he had no epileptic seizures and took part in everything, excelling in sports and games. We watched as Blerim progressed into a confident young man who did not need to rely on his father's help during his time with us. It was wonderful to see how proud his parents were seeing him interact with others and enjoying himself."

Taulant, who is in his late teens, has cerebral palsy and cannot speak.

"Yet," said Mervyn, "he took part in everything, and the smile on his face said it all."

This was Tauland's first time out of his house and he was able to walk around in the community with his family, as he was often left in his room on his own to watch TV.

Mervyn added: "His sister found it especially difficult to have a brother with cerebral palsy and was never seen outside the house with him. Over the two weeks we watched as Tauland and his family had the time of their lives at the centre, with his sister coming along daily and enjoying spending time with her brother."

Another of those at the club was 50-year-old Marika, who again had left her home for the first time in her life to come to the day care project. The team were delighted by her enthusiasm and excitement as she threw herself into everything going on.

The event finished with a ceremony where each member was presented with a certificate of achievement. Before they set off back home, they went to the park in Lushnje where they were treated to an orange juice and an ice cream. Although this is a common event in the West, it was very unusual then in Albania.

But one hour later, after she had arrived home Marika's heart stopped and she died.

Berti said: "Marika's sister told me she had gone back so happy and so excited by all that had happened during the fortnight."

A few days later, Berti, who oversaw the funeral with Mervyn, which was attended by the helpers, added: "There was not a dry eye in the church that day."

25

BERTI PUTS ON HIS RADIO HEADPHONES AGAIN

Because Berti had discovered Christianity through the radio, he was always keen that Albanians should have that opportunity as well.

In 2003, Trans World Radio had helped an Albanian Christian organisation, Waves of the Gospel, to set up Radio 7 in Tirana to provide programmes to beam throughout their country.

Two years later Berti was delighted to be invited to join the radio board as chairman.

Because there are so many other stations providing news, Radio 7 is 90 per cent Christian programmes and 10 per cent news.

One person who was particularly delighted by this was Peter Harrison, who had spent 23 years, firstly editing the tapes, and then sending Sali Rahmani's and Rifat Buzuku's recorded messages online via Trans World Radio into Albania. He said: "I always thought this work could be done by Albanian Christians and I was delighted when I was able to pass it on."

Mondays is Berti's only day off. But he spends many of his rest days on a three-hour round trip to drive to Radio 7 at Prush, Tirana, to record his two programmes – Words of Hope, a 20-minute programme which covers different Christian topics and goes out five days a week, plus a three-minute devotional thought for the day, which is transmitted daily.

"Even though I am very busy I am really glad God has allowed me to provide this special service," said Berti.

He knows people are listening because he bumps into friends who comment on the programmes and listeners send him letters.

Already the programmes transmit to most of Albania, but the station is planning to improve its transmission.

"I am so excited to receive the letters and my heart is full of joy about what is happening," said Berti. "God is using me on the radio in the same way He brought the gospel to me through the radio all those years ago."

Thirty years ago, at the army base, he had to put on his radio headphones and listen secretly to the Christian programmes.

Today on most Mondays, Berti puts on his radio headphones and openly broadcasts the Christian message to his fellow Albanians, who for most of their life had been told there was no God. It is on the same frequency the Enver Hoxha regime had used to put out its atheistic propaganda to its people and its neighbours that there is no God. What a delicious irony.

ADDENDUM

A lot has happened in Albania and to Berti since *God's Secret Listener* was first published in 2010. Here are some of the important events.

The Way of Peace Church in Lushnje: Berti said the church has become more spiritual and wiser. There is now a complete leadership team of two pastors, two elders and two deacons with Petrit Memushaj joining as the second pastor in 2017. He has particular responsibility for the church plant in the village of Bitaj. *(Sadly, Petrit died in March 2022).*

Although new members have joined, numbers have remained at about 120 adults worshipping each week because of continued migration from the country and also children, who have grown up in the church, have moved to the capital Tirana to study and then stayed there for work. They are expanding their children's work and have launched a Tomorrow Club, which is a new organisation now working in nine different churches in Albania by church planting through children.

The church is continuing its social outreach and is helping by providing olive trees, cows, bees and small tractors so local people can launch their own businesses, or work their own land.

Victory School: It is full to capacity with 700 children, with the back of the church providing an extra classroom during the week. They have rented land nearby and have already added a kitchen to provide breakfast for the children who have to come in very early from the villages. They give them Byrek, which is a traditional Albanian dish of baked or fried pastries made from a thin, flaky dough and filled with a mixture of cheese, eggs and spinach and sometimes meat and pumpkin.

All the teachers are better trained now with nationally recognised diplomas, while each class at the school has its own computer and TV, so teachers can teach interactively. Most of the teaching is done in the classroom as there is no wi-fi in the villages.

The school has also expanded its work giving IT training to many professional groups, including the police, nurses, doctors, medical staff and many others.

But one problem over the last few years has been Covid, which, like many other countries, has hit Albania hard and it even closed the Victory School for a time.

However, there have also been some surprises. Surprise No. 1: In 2010 I thought of an ambitious PR idea for the newly-published *God's Secret Listener*. Why not get Berti to present a copy of his book to the Albanian Ambassador to the UK as I knew Berti would be in England in October that year? I thought it was a long shot, but worth a try.

I carefully worded my letter to the embassy to talk about Berti's exemplary military record and how he was helping the youth of Albania by running a school teaching English to 700 pupils so they stayed in the country rather than join the thousands emigrating. I posted the letter and was shocked to receive a call on my mobile two days later from an embassy official asking when would I like to come with Berti to meet His Excellency Mr Zef Mazi, Ambassador of Albania to the UK.

So, on Thursday, November 18 Berti and I caught a taxi at Victoria Station and asked to be taken to be the Albanian Embassy at 33 St George's Drive, London. "I have never been asked for that destination before," said a surprised taxi driver as we took our seats. There was another surprise waiting as we entered the smart large terraced house that had been the embassy's home for only four years. My contact there was Flutur Shkurti and she recognised Berti as he walked into the embassy – they were distant cousins. Very Albanian, I thought.

We were taken to the office of His Excellency Zef Mazi at 10.30am and were impressed how simply and neatly the inside of the embassy was furnished, nowhere near as lavish as I expected it to be.

I hadn't let on in the letter to the Ambassador how Berti, a former captain in the army of the Stalinist dictator

Enver Hoxha, had become a Christian and was now the pastor of a lively church as well as a school principal.

However, His Excellency, a nuclear energy expert who had worked in the Albanian embassies in Switzerland and Austria, had done his homework on Berti and they chatted away in Albanian about the church in their country.

I sat there as an onlooker and thought of the complete irony of an English tabloid journalist sitting in the Albanian Embassy in London listening to a former Communist army officer and his country's ambassador discussing the state of the church in Albania. That would never have happened just over 25 years earlier when the atheist dictator, Enver Hoxha, who hated everything to do with the West and particularly the church, had been ruling his country with a rod of iron.

Berti and I thought we would be there for only five minutes, but we had more than an hour with the Ambassador and at the end we presented him a special signed copy of this book and he also agreed to pass another copy on to the President of Albania, His Excellency Mr Bamir Topi.

Surprise No. 2: In July 2011 Berti was invited to speak at the Keswick Convention, an annual three-week gathering of up to 15,000 evangelical Christians which has been meeting in the Lake District since 1875. He was interviewed at a number of meetings, including the lunch book club by Rachel Baughen, a Keswick trustee, in front of 100 people. Another evening Berti went to the late-night youth meeting with 350 teenagers where he thanked their parents for praying for Albania and then told his story. It went so well that they only just finished in time for security to lock up the tent at 10.30pm.

Berti also spoke at two of the main evening meetings in front of 3,500 people each time where he was interviewed firstly by Jonathan Lamb, chairman of Keswick, for just under ten minutes. The second time was by Jo Jowett, Keswick trustee, with Sali Rahmani acting as interpreter. Berti and Sali were an absolutely brilliant double act and, although they were scripted for just seven minutes, it lasted for 15 minutes.

There was absolute silence as Berti started by thanking all those at Keswick who had prayed for Albania and then gave his testimony of listening to the ECM/TWR broadcast in secret. Halfway through his story he turned to Sali and said: "This is the man whom I listened to on the radio in secret."

That brought the house down; there were gasps and then they were given three rounds of huge applause, which I am told is unheard of at Keswick. Afterwards there was a long line of people who went up to speak to Berti and it was very moving to hear so many of them telling him: "I have prayed for Albania for many years, tonight I saw how those prayers have been answered."

Surprise No. 3: On November 26, 2019, Albania was struck by a big earthquake with a magnitude of 6.4 on the Richter Scale which lasted for 50 seconds. Its epicentre was in north western Albania, but it was felt as far away as the capital Tirana, Lushnje in central Albania, Bari in southern Italy and Belgrade, the capital of Serbia.

A total of 51 people were killed, about 3,000 injured and many homes badly damaged. It was the second earthquake to hit the area in three months and was the strongest to hit the country for more than 40 years and its deadliest in 99 years. "It was a very challenging time," said Berti, "but everybody helped, including the churches."

He was part of Lushnje board of civic leaders and the Albanian Christian Alliance (the Vëllazëria Ungjillore e Shqipërise or VUSh) of pastors, including Victory School, who co-ordinated the provision of food, clothing and tents. They also visited those affected, helping to firstly buy temporary small container homes and then helping build permanent new ones.

Finally: April 11, 2022, was an important day as it was Berti's 65th birthday when he could retire as church pastor and school principal. But nothing was further from his thoughts. "I shall carry on working," he said with a smile. He has already started planning for the future.

He wants to buy more land so the Victory School can expand further with more classrooms, increasing the work in the villages plus setting up a church plant in nearby Dreng.

Berti is hoping to increase the numbers of Christmas shoeboxes from 8,000 every year to 10,000 for children in Southern Albania, where Berti is the area co-ordinator for the Operation Christmas Child charity which is part of

Samaritan's Purse, an international evangelical Christian humanitarian aid organisation.

Another goal is to build a permanent church in Lushnje, separate to the Victory School. In Bitaj they want to raise more leaders and disciples so it can become an independent church.

Hardly a quiet retirement for this former Albanian army captain, now pastor and school executive director and husband, father and grandfather.

Postscript

CLOSING THOUGHTS BY BERTI

First, I want to thank God for entering in my life and being present ever since. He has reached me, someone who had never thought much about God. He has taken me from darkness and brought me to light.

I am grateful to many people who have helped me to know God and to serve him.

I want to thank especially Stephen Bell, who has always been with me in my ministry.

I thank Gani Smolica whom God used as a turning point in my life in Christ.

I thank all the brothers and sisters of ECM, and especially Arthur Prescott, who has been very patient with me.

Thank you to Douglas Livingston who gave me the vision for Victory School.

Especially, I am very thankful to Charles Ball, Donna Rosales and others from Calvary Church who have blessed our church with their gifts of evangelism.

Thank you to Alma, Servete, and Bedrije, who have ministered in the Victory School and the Way of Peace Church untiringly.

Thank you to my son Dorian and my daughter Alta and her husband Lenci who all have a great vision for the Albanian Church, and who have given me great support and encouragement to continue boldly in building the church and who have helped me have a clear vision for the Victory School to use it in God's service.

In addition, I want to thank the foundation, Hope for Albania, especially Pier and Anette, who have made it possible that we have a building to meet in, and who have enabled our church to help people in need with practical aid.

These people are not in the book but I would like to thank:

Ron Anderson, of ECM, who has been very patient with me;

Jurgen Sachs who has had a great influence in my life and has been a wise teacher;

Steve Valkenburg who has been a great supporter in the church's community projects;

Janet King who has become a great encouragement for the Victory School and its ministry.

Co-workers Alfred Jani and Doke Dimashi, who have given much for the Way of Peace church and for Victory School, but are now with the Lord.

Last, I am thankful to my loving wife, Tatjana, who has been by my side in good and bad moments in our life and who has been very patient with me during all these years.

I also want to thank author John Butterworth, who has worked tirelessly for many months in putting together this book. I know the project has helped him continue on his spiritual journey.

My story has been His story as God has used so many different people from all over the world, some of whom I never met, as I have journeyed from Captain Dosti to Pastor Dosti. At the same time, I believe God has been with the country of Albania on its journey from an isolated dictatorship to an open democracy.

Dictator Enver Hoxha had claimed in 1967 that God did not exist. But I believe God has proved that He does exist and thousands of Albanian Christians will testify to that.

And to the readers of this book, what about your journey through life? I pray your story through life might not just be a coincidence of haphazard meetings, but that through people in the past, present and future you might meet the Living God and my Saviour.

ABOUT THE AUTHOR

John Butterworth has been a journalist for 44 years, a newspaper editor for 28 of those years, editing papers in Leek and Stone, Staffordshire; Shrewsbury in Shropshire, Bromsgrove and Droitwich in Worcestershire and the Black Country. In May 2008 he was awarded the MBE for services to journalism and charity after his papers raised more than £5 million for local causes. John has also been a Reader in the Church of England since 1994.

10Publishing is the publishing house of **10ofThose**.
It is committed to producing quality Christian resources
that are biblical and accessible.

www.10ofthose.com is our online retail arm selling
thousands of quality books at discounted prices.

For information contact: **info@10ofthose.com**
or check out our website: **www.10ofthose.com**